Real Estate Mistakes

Real Estate
Mistakes

How to avoid them
How to save your money

And live happily ever after...

by
Neil Jenman

The author and publisher accept responsibility
for the advice and comments in this book.

Real Estate Mistakes
By Neil Jenman

First Edition

Published by Rowley Publications Pty Limited ACN 063 990 778
25/7 Anella Avenue Castle Hill NSW 2154 Australia
Telephone: (02) 9894 8988 Facsimile: (02) 9899 8271
www.jenman.com

First Published in Australia in February 2000

Printed in Australia by Griffin Press

Design by GR8 Graphics

Distributed in Australia by Simon and Schuster.

National Library of Australia Cataloguing-in-Publication entry:-

Jenman, Neil

Real Estate Mistakes,
How to avoid them, how to save your money,
and live happily ever after.

ISBN 0 958651736

ISBN 0 958651728 (paperback)

1.Home ownership 2. House buying
3. House selling 4. Real estate business I. Title.

643.12

For Alec, my friend.

Acknowledgements

In my life, I have met so many wonderful people that to thank them all, one by one, would require several pages. You know who you are.

My wife, Reiden and my son, Lloyd, inspire me. My daughters, Haley and Ruth make me smile. Thank you Reiden for all your help.

In my real estate career, no-one has been closer to me than my friend Kerry Rowley.

The team at The Jenman Group are among the finest people in the world of business. To them, what they do is more than a business, it is a passion fuelled by their desire to change the world through ethics and client care. I thank you all for your commitment and devotion to our cause.

And then there are my clients – most of whom have become my great friends – those real estate agents who have done so much to bring ethics into real estate. These are the people with the courage to admit that many of the common systems in real estate are wrong and the character to really help consumers. They place ethics before profits. Any system rises and falls on the quality of the people who use the system. The success of The Jenman System is due to the actions of these agents, who at the time of publishing this book, number more than 300 offices and several thousand people. Thank you all for your faith and confidence in me.

My heartfelt thanks to the home-sellers and buyers of Australia. Your support and encouragement has been a thousand times higher than I ever imagined. Since the opening of our website in mid-1999, your calls, faxes and e-mails have done so much to encourage me. You are the people we all work for and the greatest reward we ever receive is your positive response. Thank you.

Neil Jenman.

Table of Contents

Foreword   xvii
Introduction   xix

PART ONE:
BUYING A HOME

Chapter One   3
YOUR MONEY
- The Danger of Debt   5
  - The First Family Aim   5
  - Buying Money   6
  - The Worst That Can Happen   6
- Your Highest Buying Price   7
  - What You Want or What You Need   7
- Four Hidden Costs   8
- Your Financial Future   10

Chapter Two   13
YOUR PURCHASE
- Your First Visit to the Area   15
- The Best Agents   16
  - Finding the Best Agent   16
  - Meeting the Agent and Seeing Some Homes   16
  - Finding the Best Home   17
- Typical Agents   18
  - Inspecting a Home   18
- Pitfalls and Helpful Hints   19
  - The First Day Purchase   19
  - The Instinct Rule   19
  - The Fed-Up Purchase   20
  - The 'Right' Time to Buy   20
  - Over-Cautious   20
  - Procrastination   21
  - The 'Rogue' Home   22
  - Friendly Advice   22
  - Professional Advice   22
  - Remorse   24
- Eight Reasons to Buy a Home   25

HOW BUYERS SAVE THOUSANDS
WITH TYPICAL AGENTS

- The Best Deal For Buyers   31
- The Betrayal of Sellers   32
- Questions Which Reduce the Price   32
- The Blame   36
- How to Buy at Auction   37
- Seven Rules for Buying at Auction   38
  - Dummy Bidding   41
  - The Reserve Price   42
  - The Fish Market Examples   43
  - The Internet Auctions   43
  - The Drama   45
- Buyers' Agents   45
- Buyer Savings   46
- Making an Offer to Buy   48
  - Are You Serious?   48
  - Show Your Money   48
  - Write it Down   49
  - Terms   49
  - The Amount of Your Offer   49
  - Two Reasons to Make an Offer   50
  - Gazumping: The Emotional Stab-in-the-Back   51
  - No Offer May be the Best Offer   52
- Investing in Real Estate   53
  - Myths of Real Estate Investing   53
  - Negative Gearing   54
  - Real Estate Marketers   55
  - Protect Yourself   56
  - Real Estate Agents   56
  - Investment Questions for Agents   57
  - Good Real Estate Investments   58

PART TWO:
SELLING YOUR HOME

Chapter Four   **63**

HOW TO CHOOSE AN AGENT
- Three Reasons Mistakes Happen   65
- The Most Wanted Person   66
  - The Quote Trap   66
  - The Price Issue   67
- How to Know the True Value of Your Home   68
- How to Interview Agents   69

Chapter Five   **73**

A SKILLED NEGOTIATOR
- 'Getting It'   75
- Skill   75
- High or Highest?   76
- The Fourth Price   77
- Auction Prices   78
  - The Case of Dean   78
  - Control   78

Chapter Six   **81**

PAYING AN AGENT
- Commission   83
- Skill, Skill, Skill   84
  - Profits of Agents   84
- Golden Rule   85
  - Discounts   86
  - The Ethics of Discounting   86
- Net Price   87

THE METHOD OF SALE

METHOD 1. AUCTION   91
- Shark Bait   91
  - The Obvious Victims.   91
  - The Hidden Victims   92
  - Your Number One Aim   92
  - The Undersell Example   92
  - Start High   93
- Appearance and Reality   94
  - Publicity   94
  - Investigating Auctions   94
  - Real Estate Courses   95
  - Auction Advertising   96
  - Anger   97
  - Home-Sellers Tricked into Auction Advertising   97
  - Conditioning   98
  - The Two Auction Traps   99
- Temptations   100
  - The 'Crunch'   100
  - The 'Stimulate' Trick   101
  - Two Reserves   101
- Deceptions   102
  - The Quoting 'Hooks'   102
  - Text-book Example   102
  - How Buyers Lose Too   103
  - Research   104
  - 'Dummy' Bids   104
  - No Bidders   105
  - The 'Date'   105
  - When Auctions 'Fail'   106
  - The 'Clearance Rate'   107
  - Buyers Do Not Like Auctions   107
  - 'Auction Areas'   108
  - Selling Before Auction   108
- Protecting Yourself   109
  - A Typical Case   109
  - The Real Estate Institute "Guarantee"   111
  - Knowledge and Advice   112
  - Let the Agent Take the Risk   112

METHOD 2. OPEN LISTING   **115**
- Low Sale   115
  - Buyers Shop Around   116
- No Sale   116
- Guarantee   117

METHOD 3. MULTI-LIST   **119**
- Best Buyers With the Worst Agent   119
- The Demise of Multi-List   120
- Multi-List Areas   121
- Conjunctions   121

METHOD 4. PRICE RANGES   **123**
- Two BIG Reasons to Reject 'Bait' Prices   124
- Activity Traps   124
- No Price   125
- Time and Patience   125

METHOD 5. SELLING PRIVATELY   **128**
- Simple   128
- Three Choices   129
- Private Sale Companies   130

METHOD 6. THE SMART SALE   **132**
- Attitude and Skill   133
- Risk and Trust   134
  - Trust   134
- Price Dangers and Truths   135
  - Asking Price and Selling Price   135
  - The Price Mountain   136
- Price Levels   138
- For Buy Price   139
  - Several Asking Prices   140
- Finding the Highest Buyer   140
- The Three Outcomes   141
- Unique and Special Homes   142
  - The Hedges Avenue Example   142

Chapter Eight   **147**

PRESENTATION
- Falling in Love   149
- First Impressions   149
- The Outside Appearance   150
- The Inside Atmosphere   152
  - Natural   152
  - Minor Repairs   153
  - During the Inspection   154
- The Value of Major Improvements   155
- Exclude ALL Inclusions!   156
- Focus on Features   157
- Your Competition in the 'Market'   158
- Finding Positives   158
  - An Up-Market Agent   159
  - Contact   159
  - Your Reason   159

Chapter Nine   **161**

OPEN INSPECTIONS
- Dangerous   163
  - Cover-Ups   164
  - After the Inspection   165
  - Qualifying   166
- Restrictive, Inconvenient, Impersonal and Frustrating   167
  - Make it Easy to Buy   167
  - Lower Prices   168

Chapter Ten   **171**

ADVERTISING & MARKETING
- The Truth   173
  - Promote Agents   174
  - Impress Each Other   174
  - Attract Buyers?   175
  - Let Agents Pay   175
  - Impress Home-Sellers   175
- Behind the Scenes   176
  - The Multi-Million Dollar Spend   176
  - A World of Ego-Mania   176
  - Protecting Yourself from Advertising Rip-Offs   177
- Kickbacks   178

- Smart Marketing   179
  - Identify the Customers   179
  - Wasting Millions to Reach Millions   179
  - Incompetence or Dishonesty   180
  - The Real Cost of Advertising   180
  - Cost Versus Return   181
  - Teaching Agents   182
- Solutions.   183
  - The 'Open' Agent is the Best Agent   183
  - Courtesy   183
  - Buyer Records   184
  - Local Buyers   184
- Visible Activity   185
- Attracting the Right Buyers   186
  - Sorting Buyers   186
  - The Buyer's Road   186
  - Information   187
  - Too Much Information   187
  - Talking Signs and Windows   188
  - Simplicity   188

Chapter Eleven   191

TROUBLE-SHOOTING: WHAT TO DO...

- If You Have Chosen To Auction   193
- If You Have Paid Money in Advance   194
- If You Signed a Harsh Agreement   195
- If You Have Allowed Open Inspections   195
- If You Are Being Threatened   196
- If You Have Chosen Open or Multi-List   196
- If You Are Being Ignored   197
- If You Receive an Offer   198
  - If You Trust the Agent   198
  - The Quick Sale   199
  - If Your Agent Lacks Skill   199
  - Paid Money?   200
  - Inclusions   200
  - A Little Bit More   201
- If Your Home is Not Selling   201
  - The Agency   202
  - You are not Lowering the Selling Price   202
  - Time and Price Must Match   203
  - Beware of 'The Lemon Tag'   203

- Another Agent?   203
- Three Choices   204
• If You Decide Not to Sell   204
- The Nasty Agent   204
• If Strangers Come 'Knocking'   205
- Cutting Out the Agent   205
• If You Want to Complain   206
• TEN VITAL POINTS for Selling Your Home   207

PART THREE:
WINNING IN REAL ESTATE

Chapter Twelve   **211**

ETHICS IN REAL ESTATE

• Agent Benefit Systems V's Client Benefit Systems   214
• When You Are a Seller And a Buyer   215
- Do You Sell First or Buy First?   215
- Confidence   216
- A Summary of Selling and Buying Together   217
• Inside Real Estate (briefly)   218
- Repeating the Errors   218
- Incompetence or Dishonesty   218
- Ego and Advertising   220
- Staff Recruitment and Treatment   221
- Education and Training   223
- Ethics Education   224
- Silencing its Critics   225
• How Everyone Can Win in Real Estate   226
- Ethics   227
- Knowledge   228
Appendices   229
Further Reading   235
Notes & Reference Sources   237

Foreword

President Real Estate Institute of Victoria 1999

Since I first met Neil Jenman in 1992, I have admired his genuine concern for the welfare of the person who really matters most in real estate - the home-seller and buyer. I know how hard he works to raise the standard of ethics in the real estate industry. As a member of the R.E.I.V. for many years and its President in 1999 I have witnessed first hand the fierce criticism Neil receives from many agents when long held beliefs about the way real estate is conducted are challenged.

Now I am delighted to say that I am also witnessing the growing support he is receiving from agents throughout Australia and overseas who are determined to improve the ethics in real estate. As for consumers the support for Neil and his ideas is overwhelmingly positive even though public awareness has not yet revealed its full potential.

For too long, too many consumers have been the victims of too many agents and their systems. In many ways, the real estate consumer is at the mercy of the real estate agent. Not any more. This book provides information which will protect consumers and their families, both financially and emotionally, from the devastating effects which can occur from flawed real estate practices.

It is a book many real estate agents will not like. But as the author says it is not written for real estate agents. It is written for sellers and buyers.

At times when reading this book I felt ashamed of the real estate industry. I am also heartened however by the fact that there are many fine people in the industry who also believe unacceptable behaviours must be stamped out.

Not only does this book assist consumers it is also a positive step towards agency ethics, standards and practice. It is a must read for all consumers and agents who are committed to improving their profession.

I am very proud to recommend it.

Introduction

This is a book for consumers about how to save thousands of dollars by avoiding real estate mistakes. It is not a book for real estate agents about how to make thousands of dollars. However, if agents help consumers to avoid mistakes, everyone wins - sellers, buyers and agents.

So, perhaps this is a book for everyone.

Walter's Mistake

When Walter decided to sell his home in Sydney's Hills District in 1993, he made a big mistake.

He contacted a licensed agent who was a member of the Real Estate Institute and whose office was part of a large real estate network. The sort of agent he could be forgiven for trusting on 'face-value'.

The agent sold Walter's home for $285,000 to a 'businessman' who was the father of one of the agent's salespeople. Walter's home was then re-sold for $420,000. The same day. Not a month later, or a year or two later, but the *same* day.

Walter was 'set-up'. He lost $135,000.

Most home-sellers rarely lose as much as Walter. But, unlike most home-sellers, Walter had a disadvantage. He suffered from Alzheimer's disease and lived in a nursing home. When the agent visited him and asked him to sign papers, he didn't ask the right questions.

Walter's son, who lived in Tasmania, complained to the real estate 'authorities'. Months later, he was informed that legal action against the agent would be unlikely to succeed because Walter's *"physical and mental condition would not allow him to give evidence in the proceedings"*. Case closed.[1]

Paul and Lyn's Mistake

When Paul and Lyn decided to buy a home in Adelaide's Hills District in 1999, they too made a big mistake.

Like Walter, they contacted a licensed agent, who was a member of the Real Estate Institute and whose office was part of a large network. The sort of agent they could be forgiven for trusting on 'face-value'.

Paul and Lyn saw a home for auction. They loved it. It was their dream home. The agent said "bidding will start around $250,000", but they were experienced enough to recognise this as a common auction 'bait' called 'under-quoting'.

Their biggest fear was that someone else would buy the home, so they asked the agent if they could buy it before the auction. The agent said *"No, it must be sold by auction."* As the auction day approached, Paul and Lyn made several calls to the agent; they were obviously excited about the home.

Five days before the auction, another agent told them that the home had been sold. They did not believe it. It must be a mistake. How could such a thing happen? They were devastated.

But when they learned the selling price, their devastation turned to anger. The home sold for almost $80,000 *less* than they were prepared to pay.

Paul and Lyn lost the home they loved and the home-seller lost $80,000.[2]

Had Paul and Lyn known what was ahead of them, they would not have lost their dream home. Their mistake came from lack of knowledge, which is the reason most consumers suffer emotional and financial trauma when they buy or sell a home. But the real cause of most mistakes is the systems and the ethics of real estate agents. This book will give you the knowledge to avoid these mistakes.

Real Estate Losses

I believe the average family loses ten thousand dollars when they sell their home.[3] Across Australia, this amounts to tens of millions of dollars lost by home-sellers every year.

Most home-sellers are not even aware of how much they are losing. As you will read, the 'cover-up' of mistakes made in the real estate industry extends all the way to the top.

But they begin with the real estate agents, themselves.

Three Agents

There are three types of real estate agents.

First, there are the honest, hard-working agents; the small-business owners who try hard to do what is best for sellers and buyers.

Unfortunately, most of these agents use systems which are riddled with mistakes which cost consumers thousands of dollars. They do not intend to deliberately cheat consumers, they just don't realise that what they have been doing for years - what they were *taught* - is wrong for consumers. Their systems are also wrong for them, as most of these agents make very little profit.

Second, there are the bad agents. They know exactly what they are doing to hurt consumers. They have got their deceit down to a fine art. As one of them said, *"I have mastered the art of faking sincerity."*

These agents are in real estate for two reasons - greed and ego. They will take your money and use it for their own ends. They will under-sell your home without thinking twice about how this affects your family. And everything they do, they will justify by saying it is perfectly legal.

These agents are highly unethical.

Third, there are the best agents. In this book, you will see how to recognise them - not just by their 'look', but by their actions - what they say and how they treat you.

The best agents have a totally different culture from typical agents. They are so different, that when you meet one, you will think, *"You are nothing like the other agents."*

These are the agents who place ethics before profit. They place your interests ahead of their own. They will always do what is best for you.

The Jenman System

In February 1984, I opened my own real estate office, Jenman Real Estate.

For many years, I had studied successful people and businesses. I learned that business is simple - work very hard in the early stages, don't borrow too much money, be careful of ego, and, most important of all, give better service to customers than anyone else.

I did not like the typical real estate methods, so I used what I had learned from my studies and applied it to my real estate office. It worked better than I had ever dreamed.

By 1989, agents were visiting our office to see what we were doing. The common question was: *"How do you make so many sales when you don't do what the other agents do?"* The answer was in the question: *we did not do what the other agents did.*

In 1991, with the help of my real estate colleague, Kerry Rowley, we began teaching other agents. Soon we were holding sales seminars all over Australia and by the mid-nineties, we were teaching full-time.

We saw how some agents treated their customers (and their staff). The more we saw, the more upset we became. We could not believe that so many systems were so blatantly dishonest.

We had many arguments with agents about ethics in real estate. Some of these agents were paying us for advice and they were asking us to endorse or promote systems we opposed.

We realised we could make a real difference to the real estate industry. And so, we launched our theme - to promote **ethics in real estate**.

It was a huge task. Many agents did not like what we said. We were accused of damaging the industry. Thousands of agents refused to come to our seminars. But some agents did agree with us, saying, *"It's about time. We admire what you are doing. We will stick with you."*

Our methods became known as The Jenman System, and slowly we began to have an effect.

At the end of 1999, more than 300 real estate offices support The Jenman System which is now the most successful real estate system in Australia (in client satisfaction and sales results).

Being Fair to Sellers and Buyers

One of the dilemmas in writing this book has been the issue of what is 'fair' to both sellers and buyers. As an agent, I was deeply conscious that my duty was to obtain the highest price for the people who 'employed' me: the home-sellers. This did not mean that buyers were cheated.

The rule was simple: get the highest price possible for the sellers and find the best home possible for the buyers (within their financial limits).

I believe, from a financial point, the people who are hurt the most in real estate are the home-sellers.

But family homes are not just about finances, they are about emotions and high stress levels.

Typical real estate systems hurt sellers *and* buyers, most of whom do not have the knowledge to protect themselves, either financially or emotionally. This book supplies that knowledge.

The first part covers 'Buying a Home' and the second part covers 'Selling a Home'. It is an 'open' book. Sure, it will show buyers how to take advantage of many systems which hurt sellers. But it will also show sellers how to protect themselves from these systems.

Advising Consumers

In 1999, we released a booklet for home-sellers, *The 18 Costly Mistakes Made by Home-Sellers*. More than 400,000 copies were distributed. From thousands of calls, there was not one complaint from consumers. But many agents complained. In fact, they complained so loudly that several agents who support The Jenman System are now banned from advertising the booklet in their local papers.[4]

In response to agents who complain about our efforts to advise consumers, we make the following points.

• All profits from book-shop sales of *Real Estate Mistakes* will be donated to the 'Do the Five, Stay Alive' project, the brainchild of swimming coach Laurie Lawrence, whose efforts save the lives of many toddlers.

• We urge consumers to apply ethical tests to all agents - whether they are 'Jenman' agents or not. The purpose of this book is to protect real estate consumers and to promote **ethics in real estate**.

• Many agents are ethical and competent. These are the only agents you should choose. **Ethics in real estate** comes first.

• We ask all agents to examine their systems from the point of view of the consumer. If you offer a better service than The Jenman

System, you have nothing to complain about. Focus on consumers, not on us.

- If any agents tell you they use The Jenman System, please confirm this on our FREE CALL number 1800 1800 18.

Approved Agents

From 2000, some agents who use The Jenman System - and who meet strict consumer service standards - will begin to be known as Jenman APPROVED.

It will take an agent many months, even years, to qualify for the APPROVED status. Changing from one system to another is never easy.

However, whether an agent is Jenman APPROVED or whether the agent merely supports portions of The Jenman System - or has nothing to do with Jenman, your approval is the only thing that matters. You choose the agent who can do the best for you.

The Ethics Battle

We are often asked by agents, "How can you say such damaging things about the real estate industry?"

Our reply is simple: "How can agents *not* say such things?" How can the real estate industry continue to use systems which hurt hundreds of thousands of Australian consumers? That is the *real* question.

We love the real estate industry. But we do not love the unethical standards of many agents and the systems they use. The home-sellers and buyers of Australia deserve better.

And that is why this book has been written.

Neil Jenman.

January 2000.

PART ONE

Buying a Home

And avoiding the common mistakes of Home-Buyers.

Honest transactions are where both sides - the sellers and the buyers - are winners.

Honest people do not want to hurt others. But they do want to protect themselves from being hurt. And that's what these next chapters will do for you. They will show you how to avoid the most common mistakes made by home-buyers.

And, if you are selling a home and buying another, you can avoid all the mistakes - of sellers and buyers. You can win at both ends. For you, it will be a happy and rewarding experience.

Sell right, buy right and... live happily ever after.

Chapter One

YOUR MONEY

"Prepare today
for the wants
of tomorrow."

Aesop
(The Ant and
the Grasshopper)

The Danger of Debt

◆

Your Highest Buying Price

◆

Four Hidden Costs

◆

Your Financial Future

The Danger of Debt

The worst mistake made by home-buyers is also one of the worst mistakes made by society - *too much debt*.

A major priority in life is security, but debt rarely leads to security. Considering that a home is meant to keep a family together, it is a tragedy that the size of the debt on the home often destroys the unity of a family.

The First Family Aim

The first aim of all families should be to own their family home, debt free. Despite what accountants say about renting versus buying or about borrowing versus owning, there is one fact they rarely mention - the *feeling* of owning your home.

A young couple, who tuck their children into bed, feel better when they own their home. An elderly couple, when they place their heads on their pillows at night, feel better when they own their home. Home ownership is about feeling good. It's one of the best feelings in the world.

You buy a home to live in for years so you should think of those years. Will they be years of happiness and security or years of misery and insecurity? It depends how you handle the temptation to borrow too much. Be very careful you do not join the 'now' generation, those people who want everything today. They see loans as 'free' money. They do not see the price they will have to pay in the years ahead.

In her book, *Debt Free*, financial consultant, Anne Hartley says: *"We go into debt for any number of reasons. To impress, to build our own self-esteem, to live up to someone else's expectations, to fill an emotional void. We buy the myth that we will be happy when we have the car, the house, the possessions of our dreams. We compensate for feelings of inadequacy by showing off our possessions. We try to kid ourself and others that we are a success - 'Look at me, what I have, what I've achieved.' It's an illusion."*

Buying Money

When you borrow money, you are *buying* money. And when you buy anything, you have to pay for it. Buying money always means you pay more than you receive. You will repay $231,760 for every $100,000 you borrow (8 percent over 25 years).

These warnings about debt do not mean you shouldn't borrow to buy your home, they just mean *be careful how much you borrow*. The feeling of finally owning your home is a better feeling than any compliment you will ever receive about the size of your home.

The Worst That Can Happen

> "When you borrow money, you are buying money."

Excess debt is the hidden evil of modern society. We are rarely told about the thousands of home-owners whose lives are ruined by big mortgages.

If we earn a high income, we don't consider that 200,000 executives lose their high income jobs each year.[1] We don't hear about the huge salaries which are used to support huge mortgages and how the salaries come to a sudden halt but the mortgages keep going. (The word mortgage comes from a French word 'mort' and means "agreement until death").

One book every high income earning person should read, is *'Job loss - It's a family affair'*. The authors describe the loss of a home: *"Losing a home is so much more than the loss of accommodation. It is a loss of history, comfort, safety and dreams. A home is a family's base, the centre of its world, and the mere prospect of having to leave it generates a welter of uncertainties."*

A home is important, but what is most important is that you can keep it, no matter what happens.

It cannot be stressed too strongly: Do not over-commit yourself with debt. Buy a home you can comfortably afford.

Your Highest Buying Price

The first thing most home-buyers do is choose an area and then decide how much they will have to pay to live in the area. The danger words are 'have to'. These lead to *having to borrow* too much or *having to work* too hard to pay for what you borrow.

What You Want or What You Need

'Want-to' and 'have-to' are the first signs that you are going beyond your limit.

It goes like this: "We 'want to' live in Richville Heights which means we 'have to' pay this much."

You should work out what you can comfortably afford and then look at what you *need*. Do newly-weds really need four bedrooms, two bathrooms and a triple garage? Of course not. They *want* these things, but they don't *need* them.

You can substantially reduce the price you need to pay for a home if you focus on what is really essential to you. You can reduce your debt before you buy, simply by cutting down on your 'want list'.

Try it. Ask yourself some tough questions such as, "What could I do without?"

Instead of buying the home you *want* for $500,000, is a home for $300,000 going to give you what you *need*? Is being $200,000 better off attractive to you?

One of the best financial favours you can do for yourself is work out how much a home would cost if you bought one based on your

> " 'Want-to' and 'have-to' are the first signs that you are going beyond your limit."

needs. When you have thought about this, you can decide on the highest price you will pay for a home. Promise yourself that you will not exceed this limit and then go and look for the home which suits your needs and is comfortably within your budget.

And remember, the price you pay for a home is not the end of the expense, it's the beginning of more. So make sure you allow for extra expenses.

Four Hidden Costs

There are four groups of expenses which many home-buyers overlook or under-estimate. Unless you are prepared for them, these expenses can ruin the joys of home ownership.

1. Purchase Costs

You will have legal expenses, inspection expenses, loan expenses and government expenses. When you buy a home, people or 'bodies' you have never heard of will be asking you for money.

> "...expenses can ruin the joys of home ownership."

Take stamp duty as an example. Buy a modest family home in Melbourne for just $280,000 and the stamp duty will be $12,460. You pay more to the State Government to buy a home than the sellers pay to the agent to sell the home.

2. Inclusion Costs

There are few things more depressing than having the home you want in the 'right' area and being unable to afford the basic inclusions. Bare light globes in sockets and sheets draped across windows will be a daily reminder of your extravagance with your purchase price. Always allow a few thousand dollars for personal inclusions.

A good rule of thumb is that inclusions will cost at least ten percent of the purchase price if the home is brand new and three percent if the home is established. Do your sums and make an allowance for personal inclusions.

3. Welcome Costs

These costs will make you believe that homes have personalities, they seem to resent a change of ownership. They show their displeasure with a series of welcoming calamities to test the new owners.

The hot water system will blow up, the roof will spring a leak, tree roots will block the sewer pipes, the fuses will keep blowing because the wiring will need replacing. It's uncanny how moving into or out of a home seems to unsettle it.

If you are financially at your limit, these 'welcome costs' will really hurt you. Be warned and be prepared.

4. Running Costs

When you receive notices for rates and insurance and you have to make regular repairs, your warm feelings of home ownership will turn very cold if you can't afford the running costs. Very few homes can be maintained for less than $150 a week. That's another $8,000 in extra costs per year - on top of your mortgage payment. Make sure you allow for these costs.

Your Financial Future

Now the good 'money news' about a home. Aside from the feeling and the freedom, buying your own home will, most likely, be one of the best financial decisions of your life. If you buy within your means, you will never regret it.

> "Many people have destroyed the equity in their family homes by investing in 'schemes' such as negative gearing."

In a few years, you will owe less than you borrowed and this, together with the increase in value, will create a big asset for you. You will have 'equity' which is the difference between your loan and the value of your home.

But be careful. You may be tempted to buy shares or investment properties or start your own business. You may forget that your home is security for your family. Never risk this security, no matter what you are told.

Many people have destroyed the equity in their family homes by investing in 'schemes' such as negative gearing. If you want to invest in something, find a way other than using the equity in your home. Some investment advisers or seminar presenters will criticise these comments. But the *purpose* of a family home is to *provide a secure home for your family*. The day you make the final payment on your home will be one of the best days of your life. Make sure you experience that day.

AVOIDING MISTAKES

The important points of...

YOUR MONEY

1. Your first aim is to own your home with no mortgage.

2. A home must be kept secure. Make sure you can keep your home, no matter what happens in the future.

3. When you borrow money, remember you are buying money.

4. Focus on what you need more than what you want.

5. Make allowance for the 'hidden costs' of buying a home.

6. The day you pay off your home will be a great day. Work towards that goal.

Chapter Two

YOUR PURCHASE

"Finding
the best home
for the price you can
comfortably afford."

Your First Visit to the Area

◆

The Best Agents

◆

Typical Agents

◆

Pitfalls and Helpful Hints

◆

Remorse

◆

Eight Reasons to Buy a Home

You are ready to buy. You know your financial limits and you have set a 'Highest Buying Price'. As you begin your search, you should decide which is most important to you - the home or the price.

If you intend to live in the home for many years, make the home your major focus. It is better to pay more and be happy in the right home than to buy cheaply and dislike the home. When selling, price comes first but when buying, the right home comes first. Just stay within your financial limits.

So don't go looking for a bargain, go looking for the right home.

Your First Visit to the Area

The first thing to do is check out your preferred area. Look in the agents' windows, gather home-buyers magazines, drive around, look at For Sale signs or visit open inspections and meet some of the agents.

You may feel frustrated by agents who don't seem interested in you. Do not get angry. Remember that most agents are dealing with lots of people, most of whom never buy from them. They become insensitive to hoards of people at open inspections. They do not know who are the genuine buyers and who are the 'lookers', so they often treat everyone with indifference.

As a genuine home buyer, you will soon appreciate the importance of finding an agent who will take a real interest in helping you find the right home.

The Best Agents

The easiest and most pleasant way to purchase a home is to find an agent you like and trust, one who understands your needs.

The best business relationships are built on trust and the best agents can be trusted to find the best home for you.

However, you must be aware that agents act on behalf of sellers and it is unethical for an agent to under-sell a home. As a buyer, you do not pay a fee to an agent (unless you hire one to buy on your behalf - see 'Buyers' Agents' in Chapter 3). You will not get a bargain from the best agents, but you will get the home you want.

Finding the Best Agent

> "The best business relationships are built on trust..."

Call all the agents in the area and select the one who sounds the most helpful and professional. You can recognise the best agents; they are polite and they are interested in helping you, but they are also busy. They will respect your time and you should respect theirs. Be careful of agents until you get to know them, but don't be openly cynical or hostile. The bad ones are used to it and the best ones won't like it. You are looking for someone to help you and there is no point starting off on a bad note.

Meeting the Agent and Seeing Some Homes

Arrange to meet the agent to talk about what you want. Do this *before* you see homes. They will spend as much time as necessary to find the right home for you if you tell them exactly what you want, when you want it and how much you can pay.

The best agents will make an appointment for you to inspect some homes, usually three or four to begin with, so they can get a good feel for your personal tastes. They will go with you to every home. They will schedule times to suit you and they will make the entire process as easy and enjoyable as possible.

When you are looking at homes, you will cut your stress in half if you always take your partner with you. All the decision makers should inspect every home together. If one person has to *"go and have a look and let me know if you find something you like"*, this will frustrate both the person looking and the agent who has to be the tour guide. For everyone's sake, the best agents will insist that all the people who intend to buy the home inspect all the homes.

Take your cheque book in case you see something you like and you need to pay a deposit. Your cheque book shows the agent that you are serious about finding the right home.

Finding the Best Home

It can be annoying to be shown homes that don't suit you. So be sure to tell the agent how you feel about each home you see.

Many buyers do not know what type of home they are going to buy until they see it. They may want a four bedroom home and later decide on a two bedroom apartment. It happens like that sometimes. Buying a home - especially an established home - involves compromise. You may have to sacrifice a feature you want in a home in order to get a feature which is more important to you.

> "The best agents will search for a home on your behalf."

It may take several weeks to find the right home. It can be disheartening when agents tell you there is *"nothing around"* or the *"sellers are holding off"* or *"if I had what you are looking for, I'd have a dozen buyers for it."* But be confident that you will find a home.

There are thousands of homes in most areas. One of them is sure to suit you.

The best agents will search for a home on your behalf. You can tell them exactly where you prefer to live and they will make polite contact with people in those areas. Many home-buyers find the right home because agents search on their behalf. This is one of the big advantages of finding the best agents - they do not 'sit and wait' for homes to become available - they go looking for them.

The best thing you can do to find the right home is to find the best agent in your preferred area. This will put you well ahead of home-buyers who deal with typical agents.

Typical Agents

Buying a home from a typical agent is hard work. You may have to demand attention to get the action you need.

Many agents will tell you there is no need to call them - all you have to do is look at their advertisements. These agents would rather place an advertisement than call the right buyer. Nevertheless, if you keep calling an agent you will have a better chance of finding a suitable home.

> "Buying a home from a typical agent is hard work.
>
> You may have to demand attention to get the action you need."

Inspecting a Home

If the time of an 'open inspection' is inconvenient, request that the agent arranges a time to suit you. Amazingly, some agents won't agree. They believe that if you are a genuine buyer, you will change your schedule to suit them. In these cases, write to the owner of the home saying you are interested in buying their home, but the agent is making it hard for you. Include your phone number and ask the owner to call you. The agent won't like this. The sellers won't like it when they realise the open inspection times make it hard for genuine buyers to inspect their home.

When you see a sign on a home you like, do not approach the owner. Always call the agent. If, after several calls, you have received no response, then approach the owner, preferably by leaving a polite note explaining the circumstances.

If you are lucky enough to find an agent who will take you to see homes, it is always best to go with the agent. You can ask questions and talk together about the area while you are going from home to home.

Pitfalls and Helpful Hints

The right time to buy a home is when you find the right home. You may find it on your first day, or it may take months. But be aware of some of the pitfalls and how you can avoid them.

The First Day Purchase

Some buyers find their ideal home the first day they start looking. This makes them nervous because they did not expect it to be so easy. Consequently they hesitate and the home is sold to another buyer.

Later, after months of searching for a home as good as the first one, they realise they missed a good opportunity. Sure, there will always be another home that suits you and you will find it eventually. But be warned: If you find the right home on the first day, think seriously about buying it.

> "The right time to buy a home is when you find the right home."

The Instinct Rule

The right home for you has the right 'feel' to it. Use your instincts and be guided by your feelings. Often, the first thought you have when you enter the home is the right thought. Later you begin to doubt your instincts and you may talk yourself out of the right home or into the wrong one. The newsreader, Barbara Walters believes in the saying, *"Trust your gut."* She is right. Never buy a home unless it *feels* right.

The Fed-Up Purchase

It only takes a few weeks for you to become 'fed-up' with spending each week-end chasing agents around open inspections or going to auctions and getting your heart broken and your wallet walloped. Soon you become desperate and you buy a 'reasonable' home instead of the right home. This is a big mistake. It is better to spend months looking for the right home than years living in the wrong home.

> "It is better to spend months looking for the right home than years living in the wrong home."

If you become fed-up with looking at homes, there are two things you can do: 1) Consider another area or another price range; or 2) Take a break. Give the home-hunting a rest for a few weeks. This does not mean you give up, but don't let being fed-up cause you to make a quick decision you will regret for years.

The 'Right' Time to Buy

No matter what the season or how the 'market' is, typical agents always say *"now is the time to buy"*. It is always a good time for an agent to make a sale.

But for you, the right time to buy is when you find the right home. Not before.

Over-Cautious

Some buyers are too careful and they buy a home well below what they can comfortably afford. They spend years living in a home they don't like. These people fear the commitment of home ownership. But a mortgage is, in many respects, far less of a commitment than rent. A mortgage means you are the owner of the home (or at least heading that way) and you can come and go as you please. You can move out and rent the home to a tenant. But if you rent, you are committed for the term of the lease. One of the benefits of home ownership is the freedom it gives you.

Procrastination

Be careful not to lose too much time through procrastination. Sometimes we all need a push to do the right thing for ourselves as the following story shows.

It was 1985. The buyer was in his early forties. He had a round, jolly face and he smiled a lot. He wanted to buy a home-unit with his mother. He played the guitar in a folk-band and thought a unit was safer for his mother when he worked late. They had been renting for a long time.

"And how long have you been looking for something to buy?" asked the agent.

"Aw, quite a while now, haven't we?" he said to his mother.

"Yes, John. And I wish you'd make up your mind. I'm getting sick of this."

He replied, *"We don't want to do the wrong thing now, do we Mum?"*

"No, we don't, but this is getting ridiculous and I am getting older."

> "Sometimes we all need a push to do the right thing for ourselves..."

John told his mother that she was *"only 76."*

She said, *"Yes, but I was 61 when we started looking."*

John suffered from procrastination. In the 15 years they had been 'looking to buy' there had been two real estate booms while John and his mother had paid thousands of dollars in rent. The agent and John's mother finally 'pushed' John into a decision.

Five years later, another real estate boom arrived. John was nudging fifty when his mum died. Fortunately she had lived long enough to see him acquire a large asset.

Take your time, but don't wait too long.

The 'Rogue' Home

Have you ever noticed that some homes are often for sale? You see a For Sale sign and then later a Sold sign and then, within a few months, the home is for sale again. Why is this?

Some homes are 'rogues'. And this is not discovered until the new owners move in. Some people say these homes are haunted but it's more likely something worse. It could be noisy neighbours or smells from an industrial complex.

To avoid buying a rogue home, you should have several inspections at different times and on different days. You should inspect the home on a week-end, especially a Saturday evening. Try to inspect the home during heavy rain - the best time to inspect any home. And meet the neighbours before you buy. This way you can choose your neighbours and your home. One of the biggest rules in home buying is: *know the home before you buy it*.

Friendly Advice

You find a home you love and you can't wait to tell your relatives and friends. But these are not the people who should make the major decision for you. Unless they are going to buy the home with you, do not allow your relatives and friends to influence your decision. It is your home. If it feels right for you, buy it and show it to your friends at your house warming.

Professional Advice

These are the people you must consult *before* you make the legal commitment to buy.

If you ignore this advice, you could be in the situation Phil and Cheryl were in after they bought their dream home.

One day they noticed tiny cracks in a wall. When they sought the advice they should have sought earlier, their worst fears were confirmed - major structural faults and an expense that almost ruined them. The few hundred dollars they saved by not having a building inspection report cost them $50,000.

Make sure you hire competent and professional people to inspect a home - before you buy. And be prepared for the most negative and 'picky' list of faults you have ever seen.

All homes of more than a few years in age have faults. As long as you are aware of them, you shouldn't worry too much. It's the big faults, if any, that you should worry about. And do not insult the sellers by asking for a reduction in price because of a Building Inspector's report which lists faults that were visible when you saw the home. Make allowance in your budget for these repairs.

Be sure to contact a good lawyer who specialises in real estate. Yes, you can shop around and get a cheap lawyer, but be careful trying to get first class service at a second class rate. The legal process for buying and selling a home is too important to cut costs. If you pay a fair rate, you can expect excellent service.

> "The legal process for buying and selling a home is too important to cut costs."

What you are really paying for with a lawyer is peace of mind. If something does go wrong, you will be very thankful for a good lawyer. In her best selling book, *Your Mortgage and How to Pay it Off in Five Years*, Anita Bell said, *"I would recommend you find a good lawyer - before you go house hunting. I can't recommend enough the peace of mind their advice can provide."*

Remorse

Remorse strikes most buyers. They find the home they love, get really excited about it, agree to start buying it, and the next day they get jittery. Some buyers even feel ill.

> "You can find a reason not to do anything if you try hard enough."

It's that panic when they wonder if they are making the right decision. Could they have bought for a better price? Is the home going to be large enough? Is the area right for them? Is the street too busy? How much work will they have to do? What if anything goes wrong? What if, what if, and more what if's. They are seized with an urge to cancel.

Be careful. Most buyers feel this way. It's a natural feeling known as 'Buyer's Remorse'.

Here's what to do. Wait for a few hours and then write out a list of all the things which are worrying you. Then sleep on it.

The next day, before you look at your 'worry list', think how you felt when you first saw the home. Try to bring back that mood. The best way to do this is to write out another list, only this time, write the 'positives' of the home. You will then have two lists - your 'positive list' and your 'worry list'.

In most cases, you will realise that you are suffering from 'Buyer's Remorse' and the worried feelings will pass. If not, call the agent and make a time to discuss the points which are worrying you. Arrange to have another look at the home to see if you still get that good feeling from the 'positives'.

If you still feel remorseful, cancel your purchase.

But, if you don't feel remorse, go ahead and buy the home. Chances are it's the right decision. You can find a reason not to do anything if you try hard enough. Look at the reasons you should buy. You'll get a balanced view. Either way, you'll do what's right.

Eight Reasons to Buy a Home

Here are eight reasons to buy your own home (that you won't find in a financial report).

1. It Feels Good

Paying off your own home gives you and your family a feeling of pride and satisfaction unlike anything else. This feeling should be experienced by everyone.

2. Emotional Security

A home gives you personal and emotional security. Home is where you are always welcome. No-one can come into your home without your permission. Your home is your castle.

3. Financial Security

Saving can be hard. Buying a home is a great form of saving as each payment takes you closer to the day when you achieve total ownership. Your home soon becomes your greatest financial asset.

4. Family Togetherness

Your home is the foundation for your family unit. As your children grow, they will feel secure - because home is always 'there'. Be sure to leave the welcome light on until all the family are home each night. Homes keep families together.

5. It Occupies You

You don't occupy a home as much as the home occupies you. Your home becomes a part of you. There is always something to do at home, whether it's pottering in the garden or lying on the sofa watching television. You and your family will enjoy thousands of hours at home.

6. It Takes Care of You

When you are sad, your home lifts your spirits. When you are ill, your home comforts you. When you go away, you miss your home. When you come home, you feel that special warmth which only a home provides. There is no place like home. It is your sanctuary.

7. Memories

The word 'home' is a positive word. When you think of home you think of all the dreams, the fun and the great times. Your home has special feelings. From the scent of the garden to the way the sun enters your favourite room, your home triggers wonderful thoughts. A home is full of special memories.

8. Your Home is You

You belong at home. Your home is a part of you. It's the heart of your life, a part of your soul. It's the anchor of your family's togetherness. You, your family and your home are one.

Buy a home. Hang up a 'Home Sweet Home' sign and make it a happy home.

It will be one of the greatest joys of your life.

AVOIDING MISTAKES

The important points of...

YOUR PURCHASE

1. The home is more important than the price provided you can comfortably afford it, of course.

2. Try to find one of the 'Best' agents.

3. Take your partner and your cheque book with you.

4. The right time to buy is when you find the right home.

5. If you get fed-up, don't quit. Take a break for a few weeks.

6. Seek professional advice from building inspectors.

7. A good real estate lawyer can be your best asset.

8. Remember the eight 'feel good' reasons for buying a home.

Chapter Three

HOW BUYERS
SAVE THOUSANDS
WITH
TYPICAL AGENTS

"The best agent
for the buyer is the
worst agent for the seller
when it comes to price."

The Best Deal For Buyers

◆

The Betrayal of Sellers

◆

Questions Which
Reduce the Price

◆

How to Buy at Auction

◆

Buyers' Agents

◆

Buyer Savings

◆

Making an Offer to Buy

◆

Investing in Real Estate

When sellers hire incompetent agents, buyers save thousands.

Home-buyers are amazed at how easy it is to pay less for a home. They can't believe their luck when they see a home priced at $500,000 and the agent says the owners will accept $470,000. They think, *"Wow, we would have gladly paid more than that!"*

The Best Deal For Buyers

There is nothing wrong with wanting to get the best deal when you are buying a home. What *is* wrong is what incompetent agents do to home-sellers. They charge thousands of dollars in commissions but they under-sell the homes. They make it easy for buyers to get bargains.

To buy a bargain or pay less than you are prepared to pay, you will need to find an incompetent agent. You might not be treated well, but you will often get a lower price.

You may wonder why, if agents get a percentage of the selling price, they under-sell homes so often. The answer is simple: It requires little effort to make sales when prices are low. Also, an extra $10,000 on the price means as little as $100 to the salesperson. *"Just sell it and get the commission"*, is the attitude of most typical agents. A sale means commission and no sale means no commission. It's a get the sale at *any* price attitude.

The Betrayal of Sellers

One of the biggest complaints made by home-sellers is that agents seem to work for the buyers instead of the sellers. When it comes to respecting the privacy of the sellers, some agents are more than incompetent, they are negligent. Incompetent agents betray sellers.

The first thing buyers notice about incompetent agents is how they speak about the sellers and their homes. One buyer explained it simply when she said, *"The agents are such blabber mouths."*

These agents will openly state that a home is "over-priced" or that the sellers are "unrealistic". Many an agent has been caught by home-sellers who have sent a friend to enquire about their home. When the sellers discover how the agents talk 'behind their backs', they are furious.

And the buyers are amazed. Many buy cheaply, but they would never choose the same agent when they sell. They cannot respect agents who betray sellers.

Questions Which Reduce the Price

If you want to reduce the price, you can start by asking an incompetent agent just four questions.

1. *"Why are they asking this price?"*

You don't have to say anything else. This question immediately puts the agent in the position of having to defend the price. And, if the agent is concerned about the price - as most of them are - you will often be given a reduction. The response is likely to be, *"Well, it's a bit dear, I know. But they will listen to offers."*

You can use this question for any product. It doesn't have to be real estate. No matter what you want to buy, you can ask the *reason* for the price. It works in dress shops. It works in hotels. It works everywhere. All you say is, *"Why are you asking this price?"* And, if there is any chance of a reduction, you will get it.

Incompetent agents assume that a question about price means the price is too high. As most agents want to lower the price to make a sale, they will admit that the price is high. They will try to get it cheaper for you. They won't realise that you may buy at the price being asked. Buyers often say the reason they didn't pay more for a home is that *"the agent didn't ask for more."*

> "The longer a home has been for sale, the more likely it is to sell for a lower price."

However, the best agents answer this question by saying: *"They are asking this price because… [points out the positive features - location, condition and so on]."* End of answer.

2. "Why are they selling?"

This is where incompetent agents reveal the sellers' confidential reason for selling. The answer will be something like, *"Oh, they are getting divorced,"* or *"They are in a bit of financial trouble,"* or *"They have bought something else and they need to sell this to pay for the other place."*

It almost defies belief that a professional person would reveal such details. When you know that the sellers are forced to sell, who can blame you for offering a lower price?

The best agents answer this question by saying: *"They are selling for personal reasons but I know they are serious."* End of answer.

3. "How long has it been For Sale?"

The longer a home has been for sale, the more likely it is to sell for a lower price. The perception is that the owners will be getting desperate and will accept a low offer. Often this is true. But the incompetent agent will answer this question by saying something like, *"Oh, it's been on the market for a while but they will listen to offers now."* The sellers are again made vulnerable to a low offer.

The best agents will answer this question by saying, *"It has been for sale for six weeks (or however long) but we don't expect it to be for sale much longer."* The sellers are protected.

4. "What will they take?"

This is where incompetent agents really cost sellers thousands. Their answers to this question can be incredibly negligent.

> "Incompetent agents always reveal the sellers' lowest price..."

Assume the home is priced at $250,000. One of the most common responses goes something like this: *"Oh, they did have an offer of $230,000 which they accepted, but the buyers found something else, so I know you can get it for $230,000."*

If the home is what you want and you can afford $250,000, the agent has just handed you at least $20,000 of the sellers' money.

Incompetent agents always reveal the sellers' lowest price in response to the *"What will they take?"* question.

The best agents will answer this question by saying: *"Well, I know they will take the asking price. Do you want to buy it?"*

These four questions show how incompetent agents under-sell homes. As a buyer, you can ask many more questions. Agents will keep giving you information which helps you.

More Examples

• *Have the owners had any offers?*

Incompetent agents will give you the full story on all previous offers. Be careful. Many agents also tell lies about offers and other buyers. An agent who does the wrong thing by the sellers will not be likely to do the right thing by you.

- *How much were the offers?*

This is where you will hear specific prices.

- *Are you a good judge of the market in this area?*

This is a question for the egotists. They are so quick to answer that they won't expect the next question.

- *Who put the price on this home?*

If the home is highly priced, the incompetent or egotistical agent will start blaming the owners for being 'too greedy' or 'unrealistic'. It's at this point that you realise that an incompetent agent is a home-seller's worst enemy.

- *What did you use for a comparison with this house?*

The agent will give you prices of sales in the area. This is helpful information. You can note the addresses and 'drive-by' to compare.

If you suspect the agent is being untruthful about the selling price of other homes, you can ask the person who lives in the home - either the seller who has just sold or the new owner who has just moved in. Knock on the door. Explain your situation and politely ask for help. Most sellers and buyers will be eager to tell you of their experiences. They are keen to help others avoid some of their mistakes.

- *How much do you think it will sell for?*

By this time, the agents may tell you exactly what they think the home should sell for. You will be delighted if the price is less than you were willing to pay. This scenario happens often.

- *What would you pay if you were the buyer?*

The egotists will love a chance to show how clever they are. You are likely to get an answer that starts with the words, "*Oh, if it was me, I wouldn't pay more than...*"

35

- **When do they want to move out of the house?**

The answer to this question tells you if the sellers have a deadline. In negotiation, if you can discover the other person's deadline, you have a huge tactical advantage.

- **What inclusions are they leaving behind?**

The common answer is, *"Everything stays."* The agent therefore gives away any bargaining tools the sellers may have had. When all inclusions are staying, the price of the home is the only thing left with which to bargain.

The Blame

Sellers often blame the buyers for low offers. But, as a buyer, what do you do when an agent suggests a low offer? You don't say, *"Oh no, I insist on paying more."*

> "Incompetent agents give the sellers almost no chance of the best price."

Buyers can't be blamed for low offers. Incompetent agents are to blame. Their lack of skill costs sellers dearly. Incompetent agents give sellers almost no chance of getting the best price. Many buyers feel sorry for the home-sellers when they see what agents are doing to them.

As more sellers realise the huge cost of incompetent agents, they will choose better agents. And then sellers will get higher prices and buyers will still get what they want - the right home at a price they can afford.

And that's how it should be.

How to Buy at Auction

Although you are likely to buy for much less than your limit at an auction, the problem you face is getting agents to tell you the truth about the price. If you have a limit of $320,000, the agents will entice you to homes where the owners want $350,000 by telling you that " *You might get it for $300,000.* "

Most auction agents will have no qualms - and no conscience - about forcing you to pay more than you can afford to pay. If you have to go over your limit and the sellers have to go under their price, most agents won't mind. They will hurt both you and the seller.

Aside from the emotional disappointment and the anger at being misled, there is also the financial loss to buyers from auctions.

You should obtain a building inspection report on any home you are considering. You should also obtain legal advice. The cost of these services will be a total waste if the agent has misled you about the price of the home, so be careful.

> "Someone always loses at auction."

As one ex-auction agent commented: *"One of the worst things about auctions is that people always lose money. Aside from sellers selling too cheaply, the buyers who miss out on the home all lose money for searches, inspections and legal advice. Someone always loses at auction."*

When an agent gives you an estimate of the selling price for an auction, ask for it to be confirmed in writing. The agent will say this is not practical as they do not know how high the price may go. But it is not the height of the price you are concerned with, it's whether or not the owners will ever consider selling for the low price you are being quoted.

According to several lawyers, under-quoting is illegal. In many cases, it is deliberate fraud. If you suspect fraud, or you attend an auction and fraud is evident, you should contact the fraud section of your state's Police Service. If more consumers notified the Police of fraud, other consumers would be spared the huge cost of these frauds.

Seven Rules For Buying at Auction

If you don't know the tricks used at auctions, you are certain to get hurt. Most auction agents have no regard for your feelings. They want a sale and they don't care who they hurt.

If you are inexperienced at home buying, you should avoid auctions altogether. The financial loss of a few hundred dollars on wasted inspections is bad enough, but it is nothing compared to the emotional damage of discovering that the home you love was *never* in your price range.

If you want to take the risk, here are seven rules to protect yourself and minimise the damage.

Rule 1. Believe nothing and check everything

With auctions, always assume the agents are lying to you. Sure, some may tell you the truth, but if you treat everything they say with suspicion, you won't be as easily hurt. There are so many lies told that you can't afford to believe anything until you have checked it out thoroughly.

Rule 2. Understand the 'quoting' lies

Experienced buyers know that agents under-quote the selling price by about 20 percent.[1] So, if the agent says *"Bidding to start from $300,000"*, the price is likely to be somewhere around $360,000. If your maximum price is $320,000, be careful. You could spend money on inspections, get your heart set on buying the home and all to no avail.

If you cannot get a straight answer from an agent about the price, or if you are certain you are being misled, you can - as a last resort - ask the sellers about the price.

Unlike many agents, most sellers are not interested in deceiving you. They just want you to buy their home. They do not want you to be misled or to lose money.

You can write to the sellers at the home. If the home is vacant, you can write to them care of their lawyer. Ask the agent for a copy of the contract of sale. The owners' details will be displayed. There is a sample letter for this purpose in the Appendix. If you receive no reply do not attend the auction.

Rule 3. Tell the agent nothing of importance

If you don't feel comfortable with the agent - and the chances are that you will never feel comfortable with an auction agent - tell them almost nothing. Just ask questions. Be strong. Answer any questions by saying, *"We are not sure what we intend to do."* Be vague. Use expressions such as 'maybe' or 'might' or 'perhaps' or 'we are unsure'.

Just remember that this is the person who will deliberately mislead you before the auction with the quote, at the auction with fraudulent bids and after the auction by telling you how 'lucky' you are. You can't afford to trust such agents.

Rule 4. Know the true value

The time and cost of basic research can pay handsomely. Obtain the sales details of similar homes in the area. In Melbourne and Sydney you can purchase inexpensive 'post-code' price guides [Call (02) 8268 8200 in Sydney or 1800 817 616 in Melbourne]. Similar information is also available in most areas through local councils.

If you feel you have a good chance of buying the home, you should consider contacting a registered valuer for an accurate and unbiased opinion. The money spent on a valuation is well worth the risk. Contact the Australian Property Institute (details in Appendix).

It would be far easier for everyone if all homes had an independent valuation before they were sold. Both sellers and buyers would have the benefit of independent and unbiased information.

However, a valuation, while unbiased, is still only a guide. If you love the home you might willingly pay more than the 'value'. But at least you have the benefit of a valuation on which to base your decision.

Rule 5. Get legal advice

> "Good lawyers are great value when buying a home."

Some home-buyers try to save hundreds of dollars and in doing so they risk thousands. Don't let this happen to you. If you are keen to buy a home at auction, consult a lawyer before you sign anything or spend any money. A home costs hundreds of thousands and a lawyer costs hundreds. And remember, the last person to take advice from about a real estate auction is the auction agent. You can have your lawyer speak to the agent on your behalf. Some lawyers will even accompany you to the auction. Good lawyers are great value when buying a home.

Rule 6. Do not bid too soon

The most important rule at an auction is NEVER BID UNTIL THE PROPERTY REACHES RESERVE. Until then, it is not for sale and it makes no sense to bid on anything that is not for sale. No matter how much pressure you receive, do not play into the agent's hands by bidding too soon.

Dummy Bidding

Agents are so desperate for early bidders, they will do anything to get the bidding up from its low beginning.

Some will plant dummy bidders in the crowd. Or pay 'dummy bidders' to pretend to be buyers. Others will just 'pull' bids from walls or trees. This is fraud. It is justified by the use of a thin legal line known as 'the vendor's bid', which means that a seller has the right to bid on their own home provided that the auctioneer declares this - which is almost never done. Even if the auctioneer does declare the vendor bid, 'dummy bids' are never declared.

> "Dummy bids are a central part of the auction system."

The television program, Money,[2] once did an expose` on dummy bidding. Hidden cameras filmed an agent boasting how he paid dummy bidders. Later, a reporter asked him if he ever paid dummy bidders. His answer was *"No. Never"*. The TV program showed two scenes - one with him proudly describing his deceit and the other with him denying it publicly.

Dummy bids are a central part of the auction system, despite the denials of agents and Real Estate Institutes.

But dummy bidding stops once the home reaches the reserve price and is 'officially' for sale. And that is the only time you should bid.

The Reserve Price

The reserve price is the lowest price the agents have been able to 'crunch' sellers into accepting.

And this is where auctions really favour you as a buyer. You will know the sellers' lowest price, but no-one knows your highest price.

With the attention on the sellers' lowest price, buyers save thousands at auctions.

Rule 7. Keep your highest price a secret

Once the home reaches the sellers' lowest price (the reserve), it is going to be sold to the highest bidder. Let's say $320,000 is the reserve and your highest buy price is $350,000. Under no circumstances will you exceed your highest price (you can't afford to).

> "Thousands of buyers are paying thousands of dollars below their highest prices at auctions."

But you are very likely to be the highest bidder long before you reach your highest price. If there is another bidder whose highest price is $330,000, then you will buy the home at the next bid above $330,000 which will most likely be $331,000. And you will save $19,000.

Thousands of buyers are paying thousands of dollars below their highest prices at auctions. All because the agents do not understand the principles of negotiation. As one buyer said, "It is like stealing money from the sellers. Why do the agents let this happen?"

The losses for sellers and the wins for buyers are caused because the auctions start at a low price instead of a high price. And when something starts low, the chances are that it will finish low - or at least lower than it would have finished if it had started high.

The Fish Market Examples

The fish market sellers are not so foolish as to auction fish by starting at a low price. They start with a high price and work their way down. When asked why they do this, one fishmonger gave a simple answer: *"We get the highest price when we start high. We are not so stupid that we would start low."*

The Internet Auctions

To understand how keeping your highest price a secret saves you money, check the Internet auctions at www.ebay.com or www.sold.com where you can bid 'on-line' for millions of items. The principles are *exactly* the same as a real estate auction.

The buyers have a highest price and a seller has a lowest price (the reserve).

The buyers transmit their highest price to the auction site, but it is kept a secret (just as you keep your own highest price a secret at a home auction).

The auction site bids for you by increasing your bid in stages above other bids.

Unless other bidders push the price to your highest amount, you only pay an amount which beats the bidder below you.

The illustration on the next page is an extract from an e-mail which shows the following:

- A buyer submitted a maximum bid of $127.00.
- There were a total of 10 bids.
- The final price that the item sold for was $41.00.

————Original Message————
From: aw-confirm@ebay.com <aw-confirm@ebay.com>
Date: Sunday September 12 1999 9:21 am
Subject: eBay End of Auction - Item # 157967678

Your maximum bid was in the amount of: $127.00
Final price: $41.00
Auction ended at: 09/11/99 14:38:40 PDT
Total number of bids: 10

The bids were in amounts of one dollar, so when the $127.00 maximum bid was made, the highest bidder at that stage was a person who bid $40. The price then went up by one dollar and the item was sold for $41.00 - well below the buyer's maximum of $127.00.

The same applies in real estate. Your final buying price is just a little above the other bidder, which is often well below your highest price. It's the low bidders who set the selling price for the highest bidder!

Auctions do not focus on your highest price. They focus on the seller's lowest price. Big mistake for sellers and big benefit for buyers. This is why agents who have studied negotiation and who are acting in the best interests of sellers, will not do auctions to them.

Follow the **Seven Rules** for buying at auction and one of three things will happen to you:

1. You will *miss out* on the home because there is another bidder who will pay more than your highest price; or the sellers' lowest price was too high for you. This is the worst that can happen.

2. You will buy the home at *exactly* your highest price.

3. You will buy the home for *less* than your highest price. If you follow the seven rules, this result is highly likely. Despite the hype about prices going up at auction, most buyers pay less than they intended to pay.

The Drama

Now that you know the rules for buying at auction, what will you do? Only four percent of buyers nominate auction as their preferred method of purchase. Most buyers can't be bothered with all the drama.

What you really want, as a home-buyer, is a lovely home at a price you can afford. If the right home is the most important thing to you, save yourself a lot of emotional trauma and avoid auctions. Find the best agent, pay the price you can afford; and buy the home you love.

Buyers' Agents

A Buyers' Agent ['Advocate'] works for buyers. To many people, this is a reasonable idea. If the sellers hire an agent to find a buyer at the highest price, buyers should hire an agent to find a home at the lowest price. (In the United States it is common to have Sellers' Agents and Buyers' Agents).

Buyers' Agents know how easy it is to buy homes for low prices. Many are ex-Auction Agents, who are now upsetting their old compatriots.

One Melbourne agent[3] wrote to eighteen other agents urging them to "blacklist" a Buyers' Agent for using "controversial tactics". These "tactics" included asking auctioneers to identify if their bids were fraudulent (dummy bids). The auction agent said, "This damages the auction system".

But as one home-buyer said, *Agents sure get angry when they are caught cheating*".

Buyer Savings

The most important factor in buying a home is to never exceed your financial limit. The next most important factor is the home itself. Never buy a home unless you like it. (The only exception is a first-home which may be a stepping stone to something better later). Here are three typical examples of how buyers save thousands at auctions.

Saved $193,000

• An experienced home-buyer hired an agent to purchase a five acre block of land which was scheduled for auction. The buyer's highest price was $900,000. The seller's lowest price (the reserve) was $650,000. The buyer paid $700,000 plus a $7,000 fee to the Buyers' Agent, making a 'net' saving of $193,000. The seller's agent said that it was magnificent to see the seller get $50,000 above 'reserve'. He didn't understand what happened.

Saved $255,000

• A Victorian Private School wanted to purchase a large home close to its grounds. The school hired a Buyers' Agent and gave him written instructions to pay "up to $950,000". The home was auctioned and sold to the school for $695,000. They saved $255,000.

Saved $83,000

• A Buyers' Agent who bought a home for $83,000 under his buyers' maximum said he felt terrible when he saw the sellers after the auction. *"They looked so forlorn. Their agent had just cost them $83,000. But what could I do? I was the highest bidder at a public auction. No buyer ever pays more money than they need to pay. Auctions focus on the lowest the sellers will accept not the highest the buyers will pay. This gives buyers a huge advantage."*

Agents who promote auctions as the "best way to sell" either do not realise what they are doing or they are deliberately doing the wrong thing to their sellers. It is either incompetence or dishonesty.

One agent summed it up. *"There are three groups of people involved in auctions. The agents, the buyers and the sellers. They win in that order. Agents win all the time. Buyers win many times. And sellers rarely win."*

Home-sellers rarely ask for auctions. The agents tell them it's "the best way". But the truth is that auctions are the best way for the agents, not the home-sellers. The auction system is the greatest fraud perpetrated upon Australian home-sellers by real estate agents in the past 100 years.

While ever real estate auctions exist, the agents who use them will keep winning and their sellers will keep losing. Buyers, when presented with such blatant opportunities to save thousands of dollars, cannot be blamed for buying at auction. The blame belongs with the auction agents.

Sellers and buyers all want a fair deal. But, because of typical agents and their systems, it is rare that sellers and buyers are both winners when a home is sold at auction. There are always losers at auctions.

> "...auctions are the best way for the agents, not the home-sellers."

With auctions you are dealing with a system designed to deceive you. You have to protect yourself - not by being dishonest but definitely by being guarded and perhaps a little shrewd.

Making an Offer to Buy

An offer to buy a home means you are moving from the 'interested' stage to the 'serious' stage, so treat everything seriously. The one thing you should always do, no matter how you have been treated or with whom you are dealing, is be fair (and firm). If you play games, you will antagonise the sellers and you may lose any chance of buying the home. The worst thing you can do in negotiation is to make the other side angry. When two parties become hostile, negotiations break down.

Are You Serious?

The most important message you can convey when you are ready to buy a home is that you are serious and that you can be trusted.

> "Offers in writing are far more powerful than verbal offers."

Agents do not like buyers who say, *"Give them an offer and if they accept let me know."* This does not make the agent or the sellers feel confident. Picture it from the sellers' point. What would make you take notice of an offer on your home? The answer is a serious buyer. The buyers who buy well are those who make sellers think, *"We don't want to lose these buyers."* So, if you don't want to lose the home, become a buyer that the sellers won't want to lose. Become serious.

Show Your Money

Money is a powerful negotiating tool. If you pay a ten percent deposit to the agent you will have a much better chance of your offer being accepted than if you pay a hundred dollars.

Imagine you want to offer $333,500 for a home priced at $350,000. A cheque for $33,350 - made payable to the agent's trust account - or the trust account for the sellers' lawyers, is a powerful persuader. (Be sure to check that the agent is licensed before you pay any money).

Write it Down

Offers in writing are far more powerful than verbal offers. A home cannot be sold verbally, so don't make your offer verbally. You can sign a contract of sale or you can write out your offer. Always be certain to seek legal advice before you sign anything - or, at the very least, make any written offer subject to you receiving independent legal advice. Despite any encouragement - such as cost savings - never use the same lawyer as the sellers.

Terms

Find out if there is anything you can do to assist the sellers. If you can offer the sellers favourable 'terms' you can often receive some compensation in the price.

For instance, if the sellers want to stay in the home for a few more weeks, you could allow them to 'rent' back from you. Perhaps the sellers intend to make repairs which you could offer to do. Look for anything that could be an incentive to accept your offer.

The Amount of Your Offer

Be very careful with the amount of your offer. Some people seem to think that offers involve a series of trips 'back and forth' - the buyers make an offer, the sellers reduce a bit, the buyers make another offer and so on, until both sides agree. This does happen, but it is fraught with danger. You can lose the home or you can lose trust - or both.

If you make an offer and you say, *"This is the most I will pay"*, and the agent presents your offer to the sellers who say 'no', what do you do then?

If you increase your offer - the agent who told the sellers, *"They won't pay any more"*, looks really incompetent. This upsets agents and makes sellers very suspicious. After all, you said you would *not* pay more and then you did pay more. You have lost the advantage of being seen as trustworthy.

If you intend to increase your offer later, never say *"This is my best offer."* Just say *"This is my offer"*. And then put it in writing and leave a cheque as a deposit. Be sure to include a reasonable time limit by which you require a decision. This will prevent the negotiation dragging on too long. Three working days is ample time for an offer to be considered.

Some buyers say to agents, *"We will pay $470,000 but we want you to offer $450,000 to start with."* Agents have an ethical duty to the owners and although some agents submit offers which are lower than they actually receive, this is highly unethical and even illegal.

Two Reasons to Make an Offer

There are only two reasons you should make an offer. First, if you cannot afford the asking price. In this case, the question the sellers may ask is, *"Why did you look at our home if you can't afford to buy it?"*

> "Why did you look at our home if you can't afford to buy it?"

Second, if you feel the home is too highly priced and you are prepared to risk not buying it by making a lower offer. This is quite common and quite reasonable. If you have done your research you will know the value of homes in the area. When you see the home you want, you have to decide how much you want it. The more you like it, the more you will have to be prepared to pay. The less you like it, the more you can risk losing it.

If you want to buy the home but you are not prepared to pay the asking price, then make your best offer in the beginning and say that it is your final offer. Make sure you mean it.

And, here's a tip that can help make your offer more believable - make sure the amount of your offer does not end in a 'thousand figure'. Have it end in a 'hundred figure'. It increases the chance of acceptance if you offer $333,500 instead of $333,000. It sends the message, *"This really is my maximum."*

Gazumping: The Emotional Stab-in-the-Back

If another buyer makes a higher offer than your offer and the sellers sign a contract with this other buyer - *without notifying you* - then you have been gazumped.

There is a lot of misinformation about the term 'gazumping'. Selling a home to another buyer does not mean you have been gazumped if you have been given *a chance to increase your offer*.

Gazumping occurs when you are <u>not</u> given the chance to increase your offer and the home is sold 'behind your back'. Emotionally, this is a real stab-in-the-back.

Until the sellers have signed a contract accepting your offer, they are not legally obligated to sell to you.

Here are **three ways to avoid the pain of being gazumped:**

First, accept that nothing is definite until the sellers sign the contract.

If you have made your best offer, then all you can do is hope that the sellers accept your offer and that they sign the contract quickly. Until then, you sweat.

> "...nothing is definite until the sellers sign the contract."

Second, create the opportunity to match (or better) an offer from another buyer. Write the agent a letter stating your concern about 'gazumping' and ask that you be told if another buyer makes an offer. Make sure the agent signs a copy of your letter. (A sample letter appears in the Appendix).

This is where 'bluffing' can really hurt you. If you tell the agent that your offer is your best (and final) offer, then you cannot blame the agent (or the sellers) for believing you, and selling to another buyer who offers more.

Third, offer the full asking price.

While it is still possible for you to be 'gazumped' if you agree to pay the asking price, it is less likely. Gazumping is often done because the buyers have offered too low a price and the sellers feel the buyers are being unfair. In such cases, they may welcome the chance to sell to another buyer and may not even consider informing the first buyers - especially if the low offer was said to be their "best" - one of those 'take it or leave it' type offers.

> "Gazumping is often done because the buyers have offered too low a price."

Gazumping often occurs if a home is priced too low. Why else would other buyers offer more money? Some agents say that auctions prevent gazumping, but more buyers get the emotional knife-in-the-back with auctions than with gazumping.

An agent has an obligation to obtain the highest price possible for the sellers. If there is more than one buyer interested in a home, the agent should give all buyers the chance to offer their highest price. Whoever offers the highest price becomes the buyer. For an example of how this is done fairly, see page 142 (The Hedges Avenue Example).

The emotional pain of gazumping comes when buyers are led to believe that the home is 'theirs', and it's not.

When you are buying a home, it is *never* 'yours' until the sellers sign a legally binding contract with you.

No Offer May be the Best Offer

If you really love the home and you can comfortably afford the asking price, there is a strong case to be made for *not* making an offer. Just say, *"We love your home and rather than making you an offer, we thought - because we can afford it - that we'd just like to buy it."* It will certainly make the sellers realise you are fair, plus you eliminate the risk of losing the home you love through gazumping.

If you treat people fairly you stand a better chance of receiving fair treatment in return. Buying a home is a big decision. Think it through carefully and don't be afraid to ask for advice from an independent person. Treat everyone the way you would like to be treated. Do all this and you will make your home-buying experience as pleasant as possible.

No matter how much you pay for your home, if you love it and you can afford it, you can look forward to many happy years. Owning a home is a wonderful experience. Don't risk losing it.

Investing in Real Estate

This is not a book about real estate investment. It is a book about how to avoid mistakes with your greatest asset - your family home.

However, this section will give you some brief but very important advice about the *dangers* of real estate investing.

When you learn to avoid real estate mistakes, selling or buying a home becomes a pleasant experience. Your knowledge gives you confidence and you may want to be a landlord.

If so, you must proceed with **extreme caution**.

Myths of Real Estate Investing

Real estate investing is filled with myths.

The myths begin with stories of fortunes. 'The couple whose apartment trebled in value.' 'The thirty year old who built a million dollar empire.' 'People are making thousands. And you can too.'

The 'sell' messages are all similar - real estate always goes up, the returns are guaranteed, the price will never be cheaper, now is the time to buy, you will save tax - *"The taxman pays for it"*.

But real estate doesn't always go up. It often goes down. As Financial Planner and best-selling author, Noel Whittaker says, *"Where there is the chance of a capital gain, there is also the chance of a capital loss."*[4]

Negative Gearing

You can lose your family home because of negative gearing.

It starts like this: You borrow money on your home for an 'investment' property. You have loan payments higher than the income you receive. You deliberately create a loss. And this loss is your 'tax deduction'.

Well, so are most losses - most companies that go broke do so for one reason: *too many tax deductions*. Families go broke for the same reason. Tax deductions mean losing money and losing money means you are going broke. And you should never - that's never ever under any circumstances - place your family home at risk, no matter what a seminar speaker or a real estate agent tells you. Never ever.

For thousands of people, real estate investing starts with a dream and a big 'sell'.

But here's how it can end:

You have enormous expenses. Your tenant stops paying or moves out which means no income. The bills mount up, so you lower the rent because *anything* is better than nothing. The rent goes down and your loss goes up. And it's a constant loss, it's happening every week.

And then, if the unthinkable happens and you lose your salary and either can't find another job or have to accept a lower salary, your losses become unbearable. Those tax deductions become lifestyle deductions. You decide to sell. And - shock horror - you discover that your investment is worth less than you paid for it.

If you delay selling, or if you have more than one of these 'investments' you could lose your family home.

Be careful before you invest in real estate. Ask yourself that big safety question: *What is the worst that can happen to me?* If you are not prepared to accept the worst, do not buy.

Real Estate Marketers

These people are not real estate agents. They are sales companies employed by property developers.

Despite massive amounts of bad publicity,[5] people are still being conned by real estate marketers.

Here is how they operate: There will be an inducement to an 'investment seminar'. You may be told you have won a prize. At the seminar you will hear about 'wealth creation' and 'tax minimisation'.

You will see slides of graphs showing how real estate has gone up by an average of ten percent a year.

> "...the price has been 'loaded'."

And then you will be offered a trip - probably to Queensland - where you can inspect these 'investments' which may come with 'guaranteed returns'. The salespeople will meet you at the airport, whisk you to apartment buildings, have lunch with you and by the time you are on the plane that night you will be 'stitched up'.

You will have bought a property and committed yourself to a loan, which you will spend years lamenting. Your own home will be mortgaged to the maximum to cover an amount that has been virtually stolen from you.

Some marketers are reputedly making profits of up to $50,000 per property - that's how much the price has been 'loaded'.

How do they get away with it? It's simple. They are employed by the owner and the owner can sell a property for any amount. They are not real estate agents so they don't need even the most basic license. When they are caught - which they often are - they fall back on that old real estate line: *"Real estate is a long term investment. We tell people that. You just have to give it time."* In this case, about thirty years of time.

Protect Yourself

There are three things you must do to protect yourself with any real estate investment.

First, check out the area. Visit local agents and compare the price of all properties for sale. Second, obtain an independent, unbiased valuation from a registered valuer. And third, seek **independent legal advice** before you sign anything.

Do not use the lawyers recommended by the marketing company. And do not take any notice of valuations provided by the marketers. Be careful of the special deals offered by banks which are tied to the marketers.

With many of these marketers, you are in a den of thieves. The best thing you can do is to get out of there, fast.

Real Estate Agents

Should you trust the investment advice you receive from a licensed real estate agent? Not according to the FPA (Financial Planning Association).

> "Many real estate agents do not give good investment advice."

In a submission to the Australian Securities and Investment Commission (ASIC), the FPA has made a number of recommendations which the ASIC has passed on to the Federal Government. The essence is that real estate agents be restricted in the advice they are allowed to give to investors.

The recommendations are that agents must disclose that they are being paid a commission from the sellers of the property. Also, the agents will have to disclose the financial implications of investing in real estate such as, high risk, high entry and exit costs, high maintenance and that it can be hard to turn into cash.

How Buyers Save Thousands with Typical Agents

Predictably, many agents are outraged at these proposals. But again they do themselves great harm because the reasons for their outrage are based on the benefits they will lose. They are not focussed on how the consumers may benefit. Letters are being circulated among agents urging them to "act now"[6] and write to the Real Estate Institute of Australia urging that the Government not "interfere".

If consumer benefits are examined, the FPA has a strong case - even though the agents are accusing the FPA of self-interest, because the FPA often promotes shares as an alternative to real estate investment.

Many real estate agents do not give good investment advice. Many can't look after their own money, let alone the money of consumers. Real Estate agents are just that - agents. They are paid a commission for selling a property.

If you buy a property for investment, the best advice is to seek advice from someone who is not getting a financial benefit from your purchase.

> "Real Estate agents should, at the very least, have to prove that their advice is sound."

Consumers should be protected from bad investment advice. And people who cannot look after their own finances should not be giving financial advice. Real Estate agents should, at the very least, have to prove that their advice is sound.

Investment Questions for Agents

If an agent says a property is a good investment, ask some simple questions: *"On what basis are you saying this is a good investment? If you are incorrect, will you be responsible for any losses I suffer?"*

And here is a very good question: *"Have you got a good record of investing for yourself?"* If the agent says "Yes", then ask the agent to prove it to you. You can always recognise information which is

57

embarrassing or disgraceful. It is described as private and confidential.

The message is the same - get independent advice from a person who is qualified to give it - not necessarily academically qualified, but a person with a good personal investment record and a person who has clients with good investment records.

For too long, too many agents have used the line, *"It's a good investment"*, to sell real estate without any basis for making such a statement, other than the passage of time. Sure, properties increase in value over time, but so do groceries. And some people take more care to read the labelling on grocery items than they do to check real estate investment products.

There was once a poster in many real estate offices that showed an elderly man with a walking stick and a long beard. A caption read, *"This is the young man who waited for the price of real estate to come down."* When real estate prices went down, so did the poster.

Good Real Estate Investments

There are some good real estate investments. You just need to be very careful what you buy, where you buy and how you buy. Be especially careful about borrowing too much. And never place your family home at risk.

> "High risk is for high fliers, not for families."

A safe way to invest is to simply save a deposit and find a property where you only have one loan which is secured only against the investment property.

Make sure that the expenses are covered by the rental income. This way, if anything goes wrong, you will not get hurt. It is 'set and forget' investing.

High risk is for high fliers, not for families. If you can afford it, always try to buy close to where you live so that you can watch your property and the market in your area.

This advice may be accused of being too protective. If so, it has achieved its aim. Family investors are rarely told the 'down' side. In a book written for family home-owners, your personal happiness is the major focus.

Investing in real estate is wonderful if you have low expenses, if the property is being looked after, if the market rises over time and if your loan is being paid off. That is the secret of good real estate investing. Safe and secure.

Just like bricks and mortar.

AVOIDING MISTAKES

The important points of...

HOW TO SAVE THOUSANDS

1. You won't get a bargain with the best agents but you will get the best treatment and probably the best home.

2. Ask questions of typical agents which can reduce the price by several thousand dollars.

3. If you want to buy at an auction, use the **Seven Rules.**

4. Never ever exceed your highest buying price, no matter what.

5. Be serious when making an offer.

6. If you really love the home and you can afford it, ask yourself if making an offer is worth the risk of losing it.

7. Never place your home at risk with negative gearing.

8. Always do basic research and get independent advice *before* you buy real estate as an investment.

PART TWO
Selling
Your
Home

How to save thousands
of dollars
when selling your
family home.

Chapter Four

HOW TO
CHOOSE
AN AGENT

"The biggest mistake is

choosing the wrong agent."

**Three Reasons
Mistakes Happen**

◆

The Most Wanted Person

◆

**How to Know the
True Value of Your Home**

◆

How to Interview Agents

When you know how some real estate systems can hurt you, you will be able to avoid all the mistakes which cost you money and heartbreak.

Three Reasons Mistakes Happen

Most real estate mistakes happen for three reasons: Not having enough knowledge, not thinking clearly and the worst of all - not having agents who care enough to help you avoid the mistakes.

1. Knowledge

It is hard to avoid mistakes if you lack knowledge. Real estate agents have a huge advantage - they are the experts. The agents will tell you "This is the way it is done" and if it sounds plausible - as it often does - you will go ahead and do it.

Many home-sellers, after they have lost thousands of dollars, often say they had a *feeling* something was not right. They lack knowledge, but not instinct. If you meet an agent and have a feeling that something is wrong, you are probably right. You could be on the verge of making a big mistake, so find out *why* you don't feel right. Often, all you have to do is ask a few simple questions. Check things out a little better. A bit more time, before you make a decision, can save you a lot of pain later.

2. Thinking

"I just didn't think about it," is what people often say when disaster strikes. Thinking prevents disasters and protects us from harm. The key to clear and accurate thinking is asking simple questions. When you add a little bit of knowledge to a few simple questions, you will enjoy the reaction of some agents.

Shirley from Glen Waverley in Victoria said, *"It was wonderful to be so informed. It gave me heaps more confidence. It was fascinating to watch cocky attitudes of agents (generated in part, I suspect, because they were dealing with a woman) mutate through wariness, to respect and in one case, downright crankiness! Knowledge, as the old saying goes, is certainly power!"*

The knowledge, you gain from this book plus your ability to think clearly, will save you thousands of dollars.

3. Caring

It is not the home-sellers who have the problem with caring, it is the agents. Thousands of home-sellers give their homes to agents who only care about one thing - their commission. They do not care about their clients and they do not care about getting the best price.

The best decision you can make when selling your home is to choose the best agent. And the best agent is the one who really cares about you.

The Most Wanted Person

When you are thinking about selling, you are the most wanted person in real estate. Every agent wants to be the chosen agent who 'lists' your home. Homes for sale are called 'listings' - and, to any agent, many listings mean many sales.

> "Agents who tell the truth often lose business to agents who tell lies."

The Quote Trap

If you choose an agent purely on quoted price, you could make a huge mistake. Thousands of sellers have learned, from bitter experience, that the price the agents *quote* and the price they *get* are *different* prices.

But it is very hard to ignore some agents. When an agent, who is supposed to be a professional, says your home is worth a huge amount, it is very tempting. However, most sellers forget one vital fact: *the agents are biased.* If they quote you a price and their competitor quotes a higher price, they risk losing your business.

And if they lose, they don't get paid.

Agents who tell the truth often lose business to agents who tell lies. This puts the honest agents in a terrible situation. If they tell the truth, they risk rejection. This is why they avoid the price and say: *"It's hard to judge exactly. It depends on the market. Let's not put a price on it. Let's auction and see what happens."*

Agents are terrified of home-sellers who say, "Tell me what my home is worth" and that is why they will do all they can to avoid what is known as 'The Price Issue'.

The Price Issue

Agents often say they do not know how much a home is worth. But, no matter what they say, they do know. They just do not want to tell sellers and risk losing the business.

If you demand a quick quote on your home's selling price, many agents will either avoid or inflate the price. This is not like getting a painting quote. Remember, the agent is not the buyer of your home. He or she is the person who finds and negotiates with the buyer. You are looking for the best agent to *sell* your home.

It is similar to a job interview. The job description is: *an agent you like who will get you the highest price possible and who will be honest with you.*

> "What will you do to get the best price for my home?"

The best question to ask an agent is: *"What will you do to get the best price for my home?"*

Allow the agent time to answer this question. If you demand instant answers to *"How much is my home worth?"* and *"How much is your commission?"*, instead of *"What will you do?"*, you will probably be told lies. Or, even worse, you will miss the best agent.

How to Know the True Value of Your Home

There is one excellent way to know what your home is truly worth: *Before you call an agent, call a valuer.*

A valuer is not biased about your home because a valuer has no financial interest in the value. You are naturally biased because you want the best price. The agents are biased because they want to be selected as your agent. And the buyers are biased because they want to buy for the best price. Valuers are the only people who are not biased - they get paid no matter how much your home is worth.

Valuers are highly qualified. Their's is a specialised field. But most important of all - from an accuracy point - a valuer can be legally liable for a mistake. Valuers are careful.

You too should be careful. You should have an independent valuer - *not one who works in a local real estate office* - inspect your home before you call an agent.

A valuation is a great investment for a home worth hundreds of thousands of dollars. It gives you powerful knowledge. It enables you to make plans based on facts not opinions of people who have a financial interest in the sale of your home. Every home should be valued before being sold.

Once you have a valuation - and you are aware of all the mistakes you must avoid - you are then ready to select your agent.

How to Interview Agents

Always interview at least two agents. (The only exception is if one agent is highly recommended by people whose opinion you respect).

If you do not like either agent, call a third. Keep going until you find the best agent. If you have to interview a dozen agents, do so. Do not underestimate the importance of choosing the best agent. And do not do what many sellers do - select the agent you dislike the least. Good agents do exist. When you know what to look for, you will find one.

When you meet agents, look at their personal presentation. Do they appeal to you? Do they seem like nice people? Listen to your instincts. Show each agent around your home. Watch their level of interest by seeing if they ask questions or make notes.

After agents have seen your home, make them feel comfortable and then ask the question: *"What will you do to get the best price for my home?"*

Some agents will say, *"How much do you want?"* or *"What figure did you have in mind?"* Do not answer these questions. Not yet. You are conducting a job interview. Simply say, *"Before we talk about a specific price, I would like you to tell me what your agency can do to get the best price for my home."*

Do not be intimidated or allow yourself to be pressured into doing anything that doesn't feel right. It is your home and you are in charge. You have two ways of dealing with agents. For agents you like, ask what they will do for you. For agents you don't like, just say, *"I have another agent coming soon. So thank you for coming around. I will call you if I need you."* And then move towards the front door. They will leave.

When you lack knowledge, agents can easily confuse or mislead you. But when you have a valuation and you have read this book, you cannot be so easily confused or misled.

When the agent begins his or her presentation, you will soon know if you have the right agent. If the presentation is about auctions or open inspections or if you are asked to pay money in advance for advertising, show them this book and say, *"Have you read this?"* Watch their reaction.

If their answers do not satisfy you, you have not found the best agent.

However, when you find an agent who cares about you and demonstrates this - in proof, not words - and you feel comfortable, you are ready to make the most important decision about selling your home - choosing your agent.

AVOIDING MISTAKES

The important points of...

HOW TO CHOOSE AN AGENT

1. Read Part 2 of this book before you choose an agent. The simple tips you acquire will make it almost impossible for your home to be sold too cheaply.

2. Invest in a valuation.

3. Be careful of the agent who gives you a big quote.

4. Be more careful of agents who avoid the 'Price Issue' with cliches such as, "It depends on the market."

5. Ask agents what they will do to get the highest price.

6. Interview agents until you find one you like.

7. Never hire an agent you don't like.

Chapter Five

A SKILLED NEGOTIATOR

"The best agents are
skilled negotiators."

'Getting It'

◆

Skill

◆

High or Highest?

◆

The Fourth Price

◆

Auction Prices

I n his book, *Life Strategies*, Phillip McGraw says the first law in life is, "You either get it or you don't. Become one of those who gets it."

'Getting It'

When it comes to getting the highest price for your home, most agents don't 'get it' (they don't get the strategy and they don't get the highest price).

The most dangerous people are those who do not understand what they are doing. And the most dangerous agents are those who recommend - and believe in - methods which undersell homes.

You can lose a lot of money if you hire an agent who doesn't 'get it'.

Skill

Provided a home is well priced, it is not hard to sell. What *is* hard is getting the highest price. And this requires *negotiating* skill.

Lack of negotiating skill is the reason thousands of homes are *undersold*. Ask any home-owner how much they paid for their home. And then ask how much they *would have* paid and you will notice there is a huge difference. Most buyers admit they would have paid more. Ask them why they didn't pay more and most will say, "The agent didn't *ask* for more".

Here is a typical example of how a home is undersold.

Question: *"How much did you pay for your home?"*
Answer: *"$230,000."*
Question: *"How much would you have paid?"*
Answer: *"$240,000."*
Question: *"Why didn't you pay more?"*
Answer: *"Well, it was for sale for $245,000. The agent said the owners would accept $230,000, so that's what we paid."*

Few people dispute the importance of negotiation skills in real estate. And yet incredibly - almost unbelievably - most real estate salespeople *never* study negotiation.

Many sellers feel that agents earn commission for doing nothing. But many agents do worse than nothing - they undersell your home and then they charge you for it.

What an agent charges you is not nearly as important as what they will cost you if they sell your home too cheaply.

Negotiation is not complicated. It just requires some extra thought, which is what most agents rarely do. They don't *think about* how they can always get the highest price. They simply don't 'get it'.

High or Highest?

A high price, even one which delights sellers, may not be the *highest* price. No matter how high a price appears, the most important question is: *"Is it the highest price?"*

For example, if you want $500,000, you might begin by asking $550,000. If a buyer agrees to pay $520,000, you and the agent may be delighted. But - and this is the major point - if the buyers would have paid $530,000, you did not receive the HIGHEST price. Your home sold for less than it could have sold. It has been *undersold*. You may never know it, but you just lost $10,000.

This happens every day in real estate. The agent and the sellers may be so happy with the price offered that they don't notice the smile on the buyers' faces. They don't hear comments such as, *"Gee, we bought that cheap. We would have paid another $10,000. Aren't we glad they didn't know!"*

How long does it take you to earn $10,000? A lot longer than it takes to read this book and discover how to save this money.

The Fourth Price

The secret to getting the highest price - as opposed to a high price - is to realise how most agents think. They focus on three prices - 1) your asking price, 2) what they believe your home is worth and 3) your lowest price.

The third price becomes the major focus of most agents.

Most homes are sold when sellers say 'yes' to an offer, when they are pressured to accept their lowest price.

This is so harmful for the sellers because there is a *fourth* price - one the agents rarely focus upon - and that's **the highest price the buyers will pay.**

The critical point which most agents do not understand is this: *When most sellers agree to a price, most buyers are prepared to pay more.* And that's why sellers lose thousands of dollars. Their agents are not skilled negotiators.

So, don't let the agents discover your lowest price. Tell them to discover the buyers' highest price.

The key to getting the highest price for your home is to remember three letters: **B-H-P.** Before you say, 'Yes' to an agent, ask yourself if you are getting BHP.

BHP stands for BUYERS' HIGHEST PRICE. That's what you want your agent to get. And only skilled negotiators can do this for you.

> "...don't let the agents discover your lowest price. Tell them to discover the buyers' highest price."

Auction Prices

At an auction, the seller's lowest price is called the 'reserve'. Many properties sell above the reserve. When this happens, agents claim the price is high. True. But it is *not* true to say it is the *highest* price.

Auctions make the huge mistake of focusing on the seller's *lowest* price instead of the buyer's highest price.

Take the following case, which is a typical example of how home-sellers lose at auctions.

The Case of Dean

Dean wanted to buy a block of land in Sydney's Eastern Suburbs. His highest price was $1.3 million. He went to the auction and began bidding. The auctioneer was asking for bids of $5,000 when Dean offered to make a $1,000 bid. At this stage the price of the property had reached $1.22 million. The auctioneer refused to accept the bid saying it was "not appropriate". The property was sold to the other bidder for $1.22 million.

People who said, *"It was only a thousand dollars,"* missed the major point. Dean was prepared to pay *$1.3 million dollars*. The property was not undersold by *$1,000*. It was undersold by *$80,000* which was a huge 'loss' for the seller.

The seller should add $80,000 to the agent's commission to calculate the *real* cost of this agent.

Control

Negotiation is about control. With auctions, the agents surrender control to the buyers. They even state that *"a property is only worth what buyers will pay"*, which is an admission that buyers control the prices.

The person who should be in control of prices is the agent, on behalf of the sellers. Too many agents think that 'selling' a home means finding a buyer. But finding a buyer is only the *first* stage. The second stage, which few agents can do, is obtain the buyers' highest price (The BHP!).

Only incompetent agents say a property is *"worth what a buyer pays"*. The best agents, the true *negotiators*, know: *A property is worth what they can persuade the buyer to pay.* Whatever the buyer *can* pay is what the skilled negotiator gets for the sellers, not what the buyer *wants* to pay.

Buyers welcome the chance to buy below their maximum. With most agents, this is exactly what buyers do. But agents are paid by the sellers and when agents undersell homes, they cheat sellers.

> "When agents undersell homes, they cheat sellers."

A skilled negotiator discovers the *highest price* of buyers by spending time with them. With auctions many agents do not even meet the buyers until after they have bought. Only then, when it is too late, do they discover the buyers' highest price.

In Victoria, the Real Estate Institute has a course topic about 'what to say to the sellers when they realise their home has been sold too low at auction.'[1]

You can easily discover which agents are the best negotiators. There are several *Principles of Real Estate Negotiation*. Just ask the agent three questions,

1. *"Have you studied negotiation?"*

2. *"Do you know how to get the best price for my home?"*

3. *"Tell me what you know about negotiation."*

Most home-sellers lose thousands of dollars because their agents do not know how to negotiate.

Don't let this happen to you. Make sure the agent you hire is a highly skilled negotiator.

AVOIDING MISTAKES

The important points of...

HIRING A SKILLED NEGOTIATOR

1. Don't let the agents discover your lowest price. Tell them to discover the **Buyers' Highest Price**.

2. The 'fourth price' is the one you must focus upon - nothing else. This is the **BHP**.

3. Auctions focus on your lowest price. Big mistake.

4. Test every agent's negotiating skills by asking the three negotiation questions.

Chapter Six

PAYING AN AGENT

"It's not

what you pay them;

it's what they cost you."

Commission

◆

Skill, Skill, Skill

◆

Golden Rule

◆

Net Price

I f you're looking for a cheap agent, you won't have much trouble finding one.

But remember - cheap agents can be very expensive.

Commission

An agent's commission[1] is based on the selling price of your home. It can vary from zero to six percent.

In most states, agents fees are de-regulated, which means there is no 'set' rate. It is open competition. And you should shop around - but not necessarily with the intention of hiring the cheapest agent.

Think about it: If the first thing an agent does to win your business is to cut the commission, that's usually the first thing the agent will do when a buyer arrives - the agent will cut the price of your home. If they give their own money away, they will give your money away too.

So be careful. The last thing you should look for is an agent whose first act is to cut prices.

Instead of focusing on what the agent gets, focus on what you get. A good negotiator can be worth an extra ten percent on the price of your home - even more if you are not involved in auctions. An extra one or two percent is well worth it if you get an extra ten percent.

So, be very careful. The savings you make in commission can be wiped out by the loss in your selling price.

Skill, Skill, Skill

Some home-sellers try to win both ways - by hiring a skilled negotiator and by paying a low commission. But this is almost impossible to achieve because it is contradictory. Agents who cut fees are not skilled negotiators.

Profits of Agents

A Bureau of Statistics[2] report revealed that the annual profit of the average real estate agent in Australia is less than $36,000. If they cut their fees in half (say, from four percent to two percent), they have to sell twice as many homes to earn the same profit. It then becomes almost impossible for them to make a profit because there are not enough sales being made in their area. Although, as one observer commented, *"Most agents aren't paid much because most agents aren't worth much."*

> "Agents who cut fees are not skilled negotiators."

Choosing a real estate agent is not the same as choosing a product. If you want to buy a television, you can find different prices for the same brand and then buy at the cheapest price. If you do the same thing with real estate agents - thinking they are all the same - sure, you will find huge differences in prices. But there are huge differences in their skills and the higher the skill of the agent, the higher the price you will get. The lower the skill, the lower the price. Cheap agents get cheap prices, that's the way it is.

But expensive agents can get cheap prices too. The worst mistake you can make is to *hire an unskilled expensive agent,* then pay a big commission and receive a low selling price. Now that *really* hurts.

If the 'rule' for buying real estate is 'location, location, location', then the rule for hiring an agent is 'skill, skill, skill.'

Golden Rule

There is one certain way to protect yourself from paying too much to an agent. It is to follow **The Golden Rule of hiring an agent.** If you only take one idea from this book, take this one:

Never pay any money to any agent for any reason until your home is sold at a price you want.

Be warned: Break this rule at your peril. It is an easy rule to remember, but a hard one to follow. Some agents are very persuasive. They will use every great 'line' they know, to coerce, manipulate and even bully you into paying 'up-front' fees. Some of these lines sound really good. But they are not good, they are deceitful.

Just remember that you hire an agent to *sell your property* and any agent who wants money from you for any reason, before your home is sold, is an agent you should never consider.

The main reason some agents ask for money in advance is because they know they won't be paid later when you are upset with their broken promises.

As well as not paying money in advance, do not sign anything which *commits you* to pay any money if your home is *not* sold. Some agents will place a 'caveat' on your home if they do not sell it and you have agreed to pay fees.

> "If you can't find an agent you like, keep looking.
>
> Or sell your home yourself."

If you have any concern about signing anything, don't. Seek independent advice first, preferably from a lawyer. Do not seek advice from a Real Estate Institute. Many people think Institutes are official bodies that 'police' agents. They are not. *Real Estate Institutes represent real estate agents.*[3]

Seek advice about the comments in this book. Show it to a

lawyer or an accountant - anyone who does not have a financial interest in the sale of your home.

If you do not feel comfortable with an agent, this is a 'clue' that the agent is not suitable for you. Listen to your instincts.

Gavin De Becker, author of, *The Gift of Fear*, says, *"How many times have you said 'I knew I shouldn't have done that'? This means you got a signal and did not listen to it."* It is far better to say, *"I know it"*, rather than to say later, *"I knew it."*

Follow the Golden Rule and you will be safe. Add to it by asking the agent questions about negotiating skills and finally, make sure you are comfortable with the agent. If you can't find an agent you like, keep looking. Or sell your home yourself. Place an advertisement in the newspaper and wait. That's all many agents do. (*See Chapter 7. Method of Sale Number 5 - Selling Privately*).

Discounts

The beauty of The Golden Rule is that you pay nothing until your home is sold *and* you are happy.

One seller put it this way: *"Why should I worry too much about what I pay the agent? If I get what I want, the agent is welcome to a fair fee. If I don't get what I want, I don't pay anything."*

Nevertheless, some home-sellers still like to receive a 'discount' on the 'normal' rate. No-one should blame you for trying. But a skilled - and more importantly, an *honest* agent, will never give a discount under 'normal' conditions. To do so, would be unethical.

The Ethics of Discounting

If you sold a home and later you discovered that your agent offered your neighbour a cheaper fee, you would feel cheated. Good agents do not cheat anyone.

Loyal customers are outraged when new customers are offered a better deal. Some banks do this. So do car companies.

In the United States, the Saturn car company has a "no haggle, no hassle" policy. Rather than load the price of a new car and then lower it after haggling, they say, *"This is the price."* Clients love it because they know that no other client will get a better deal for the same product.

It is unethical to offer different rates to different clients for the same service. Usually it's the hard nosed business person who gets a discount and the elderly widow who pays the full rate.

If you get a discount, the agent should offer the same discount to all its present and past clients.

This is exactly what Saturn did.[4] When they made the decision to discount their 1998 model cars, they sent a refund cheque to 14,000 clients who had already purchased a car before the discount offer was made. Now, that is *ethics* in business.

Net Price

What you receive after paying an agent is your 'Net Price'. And this is the price you must focus upon. It is your most important price. Many sellers make the costly mistake of choosing an agent based on what the agent charges.

Good agents are worth a higher fee. Bad agents are not worth any fee. Some are so desperate they will go as low as half a percent to sell your home. If they go low you will go low too. Remember - cheap agents usually mean cheap prices.

So, work out what you need, know the true value of your home and hire the best negotiator at a fair fee. This is the best way to get the highest 'net price' for yourself.

AVOIDING MISTAKES

The important points of...

PAYING AN AGENT

1. Cheap agents mean cheap prices.

2. If agents cut their fees, they will also cut your price.

3. A skilled negotiator can be worth an extra 10 percent on the selling price of your home.

4. **Warning! Use The Golden Rule: Never pay any money to any agent for any reason until your home is sold and you are fully satisfied with the agent.**

5. It is unethical to offer different rates to different people for the same service. Remember the example of Saturn.

6. Instead of focussing on what the agent gets, focus on what you get. Focus on your 'net price'.

Chapter Seven

THE METHOD
OF SALE

"After your choice of agent,

nothing is more important

than your method of sale."

1. AUCTION

◆

2. OPEN LISTING

◆

3. MULTI-LIST

◆

4. PRICE RANGES

◆

5. PRIVATE SALE

◆

6. THE SMART SALE

How you sell your home will have a huge impact on how much you receive for your home. This chapter will show you how to save thousands of dollars and avoid the enormous stress caused by choosing the wrong method of sale.

Method 1. AUCTION

Auction is the worst method of selling your home. It gives you a lower price and exposes you to tremendous risk.

You are about to discover information about real estate auctions that most agents will never tell you. But first, an obvious warning: If you want advice about auctions, the last person to ask is an auction agent.

Shark Bait

In his book, *Swim with the Sharks Without Being Eaten Alive*, author Harvey Mackay says there are three types of people in business: the sharks, the shark bait and those who are shark-proof. In the business of auctions, home-sellers are prime shark bait. But, when they understand the dangers and know the truths about auctions, they become 'shark-proof'.

> "If you want advice about auctions, the last person to ask is an auction agent."

The Obvious Victims

Thousands of auction victims know the pain of expecting their homes to sell for a high price, only to be forced into accepting a low price at the auction. These people are the obvious victims and they all tell a similar story: *"The agent told me I'd get one price, but I got much less."* As one lady described it, *"Selling my home at auction was the worst experience of my life."* She was told that an auction would *"easily give her more than $400,000"*. But, after weeks of pressure from the agent, she found herself selling for $320,000 which left her nearly $100,000 short of the figure she expected. This lady is one of tens of thousands of obvious auction victims. However, there are thousands of auction victims who are not so obvious.

The Hidden Victims

The hidden auction victims are those who sell their properties for more than the reserve price (the *lowest* price) but not for the highest price.

These sellers *think* they received a good price, but don't realise they did not get the *highest* price.

Your Number One Aim

The aim when selling your home is to get the *highest* price.

At auctions, the agents know *your* lowest price - that's the 'reserve' - but they don't know the *buyers'* highest price (the BHP).

If there are two buyers at the auction and they keep bidding, it *seems* really good because the price keeps going up.

But when one buyer reaches his or her highest price, the bidding stops. And because no-one asks the highest bidder to pay more, your home sells for much less than it should have. It has not been sold for the buyer's highest price.

Auction buyers rarely pay their highest price. With auctions, the only people who always offer their highest price are the 'under-bidders', those who miss out.

Tragically, for thousands of home-sellers, most agents do not understand what is happening; and those who do understand, deliberately avoid mentioning it, preferring instead to focus on how much your home sold for above your lowest price - the reserve.

The Undersell Example

Watch what happens and see how you, the seller, can be made to think you are winning, when you are actually losing thousands.

Let's say your reserve price is $350,000. At the auction, there are two genuine bidders.

Bidder A has a highest limit of $390,000. Bidder B has a highest limit of $360,000. These are the two BHP's.

Now, ask yourself: which BHP do you want - the $360,000 or the $390,000?

The answer is easy. You want the $390,000. But with an auction, you are not likely to get it.

When the bidding reaches $350,000, your home is 'on the market'. It is about to be sold. The bids will probably increase in amounts of $1,000. When the price reaches $360,000, Bidder B's highest price has been reached.

> "You lose money because the focus of the agent is on your lowest price."

Bidder A then bids $361,000 and your home is sold.

The price is $11,000 above the reserve, but your home sold for **$29,000** *less* than Buyer A would have paid for it. And, like most hidden auction victims, you will never realise what has happened.

You lose money because the focus of the agent is on your lowest price, instead of the buyer's highest. Had the agent been a skilled negotiator, the buyer's highest price would have been known *before* you sold. And you would have received an extra $29,000.

As soon as an auction reaches your lowest price, it begins to slow down, almost as if it runs out of breath. Soon it collapses.

Start High

The only reason prices go up with auctions is because they start low. A basic rule of negotiation is *always start high*. It is much better to start *above* the price you want, rather than below the price you want.

Auctions start low and that's where they finish - low. No matter how high they climb, they almost always finish lower than if they had started high.

One agent, who stopped using auctions, said: *"It was terrible to discover, after the auction, that a buyer was prepared to pay more money. In almost all auctions, the highest bidder would have paid more."*

The more the auction agent can keep the focus on a lower price, the more chance the agent has of selling it. And this is one of the main reasons agents like auctions - they start low which makes it easier to make sales.

Appearance and Reality

Publicity

Home-sellers lose thousands due to auction agents focusing on the sellers' lowest prices instead of the buyers' highest prices.

Each time you see headlines saying homes have sold "over reserve", always remember to ask: *"How much did they sell under the buyer's highest price?"*

Imagine a headline which said: *"Home sold for $29,000 less than the buyers wanted to pay!"* It is the *same* as saying *"Sold $11,000 above reserve."*

Investigating Auctions

A journalist with one of the major newspapers investigated the auction system. At the first auction she attended, a home sold for $231,000. The 'reserve' was $225,000. The journalist thought what most people think: *"Auctions look pretty good for the seller."* But then she asked the buyer what was the highest price he would have paid. He grinned and said, *"$240,000"*. The journalist realised home-sellers were losing thousands at auctions without knowing it. This was a big story, one that could save consumers millions of dollars.

The journalist wrote a large feature on the realities of auctions. The story was 'pulled'. In her words, *"The story was so watered down from the original (and a few things changed without them telling me) that any life left in it had been drained out."*

Real Estate Courses

The horrible reality of auctions can be seen in places consumers and journalists rarely visit - the real estate training courses.

In 1998, Kyle Watson was studying real estate at his local Technical College. He could barely believe what he was being taught.

The teacher's attitude was typical of the attitude of many agents - but it still shocked Kyle to hear such things in a Government approved course.

On the subject of auctions the teacher said to the class, *"Sometimes it's good to give the owner a kick in the guts"*.[1]

Another teacher, in Melbourne, openly recommends lying to home-sellers.[2] To get prices down, this agent teaches a common trick. If you get an offer from a buyer before an auction, always tell the sellers that the offer is lower than it actually is, which helps to 'condition' them to accept a lower price at the auction. His exact words to his students are: *"If you get an offer before the auction of $270,000, convey to the owner a lower figure, say, $250,000."*

Auction Advertising

One of the main reasons agents like auctions is the increased money for advertising which home-sellers pay. (As you will see in Chapter Ten, advertising is an enormous waste of money.)

The notes from the Melbourne course, include the following comment:

> "The amount spent on advertising is much greater with an auction.
> This means extra publicity for your company."

And this statement, which again is part of the <u>written</u> course notes:

> "If the seller is moving interstate ask who is
> paying for the advertising. If it is being paid for
> by the company, 'bump up' the overall advertising schedule."

But if the sellers have no money, the agents will suggest borrowing on a credit card or arranging a loan from the bank until the home sells. The pressure of this extra debt increases the pressure to sell, which again suits the agents.

Some agents agree to 'loan' the advertising costs to the sellers, but if the sellers wish to change agents before the property is sold - and many do - the advertising money must be repaid in full. If the sellers do not have the money they are trapped with that agent.

The notes in the training course are clear:

> "With a large advertising budget, the client will be
> loyal to you for longer. If they owe $4,000, $5,000 or $6,000,
> taking the property away from you will mean they have to
> pay the advertising money owing immediately!"

Another course says: *"How to get money from people up front."* It has a large heading: *"DOLLARS IN YOUR POCKET."* And then, in bold type it asks: ***"Is this Mercenary?"*** followed by the unashamedly gleeful answer: *"Sure is."* This course recommends placing a "charge" against the sellers' homes to make sure they pay.

Anger

The reason sellers don't pay is because they are angry and upset. And often broke. They were told that a high price will come from an auction and the more money spent on advertising, the higher would be the price. But when the final auction price is thousands below the agent's quote - or when they get no buyers at the auction - they realise they have been duped. And then the agents sue them for money which was used to promote the agents. No wonder home-sellers get so angry.

Home-Sellers Tricked into Auction Advertising

This is a typical example of something that goes on constantly with auction advertising. It is taken from a letter written by one of Melbourne's most well known auction firms.[3]

The agent wrote: *"Your home is a very saleable property and should sell for $350,000 or more."*

The sellers signed for auction. Five weeks later, the highest bid at the auction was $250,000 - $100,000 *below* the agent's 'quote'. They refused to accept this price.

And so the agent sued the sellers for $3,954.47 in advertising costs.

The agent also placed a 'caveat' on their home which prevented it from being sold until the advertising money was paid. This agent, whose first letter prior to 'signing up' the sellers, said, *"Our professional integrity will ensure the highest price for your home"*, now wrote saying: *"Your property was unsuccessfully auctioned and it is commercially appropriate that we lodge a caveat."*

Few sellers have the money to employ a lawyer to fight these cases.

A lady who worked with the Victorian Sheriff's Office[4] said that one of her most unpleasant jobs was to execute warrants against home-owners on behalf of agents for *"expenses relating to failed auctions"*. She described how home-owners were *"furious and distraught"* with agents who had misled them over auctions.

To avoid this ever happening to you, remember The Golden Rule - ***"Never pay any money to any agent for any reason until your home is sold and you are happy that the agent has done the best for you."***

Most real estate courses focus on benefits for agents, not benefits for their clients.

Conditioning

A course held by the Real Estate Institute of New South Wales was called, *"How to Condition Sellers."*

"Conditioning" means persuading the seller to reduce the price of a property. It is accepted in real estate that, *"Conditioning is easier with an auction."*

Before you 'sign up' for an auction you will be 'quoted' a high price. Once you sign, the conditioning process begins in earnest. And it continues right up until your home is sold.

> "Many real estate networks use standard conditioning letters..."

One agent's wife, who listens to her husband on the phone, said that conditioning seems to work in three stages - first, it's the good news, the advertisements are going in and there are lots of people inquiring. Second, it's the "a little tougher" news where the agent says the prices mentioned by the buyers are lower than expected. This "tougher" news will continue for a few weeks. And then comes the third stage, which is the "lot tougher" news. The auction is close now and the agent wants to lower the price.

Many real estate networks use standard 'conditioning letters'[5] to deliver increasingly bad news as the day of the auction gets closer.

Sellers who experience 'conditioning' hear some of the most misleading lines in real estate. The agents will say, *"This is what the market is telling us. We have advertised your home, we have shown it to dozens of people and they all think it's worth less than you expected."*

The Two Auction Traps

To sell plenty of homes, most auction agents set two traps for sellers. First, they persuade you that auctions get high prices. They talk about "the price going up" and tell you about past 'successes' (while not mentioning most failures). Once they list your property, the second trap is sprung - getting you *down* in price by conditioning you.

Some agents use another expression - *"managing the sellers' expectations."* It appears more 'professional'. But conditioning is conditioning whatever it is called.

Other expressions used are "crunch them", "beat them around the head", "make them sweat" and "get it through". To hear some agents in private conversation, a person could be mistaken for thinking they are describing torture. To many sellers, that is exactly what an auction is - mental and financial torture inflicted by agents who are only interested in making a sale at any price. Make no mistake: the sale, not the price, is the primary purpose of an auction.

The appearance of real estate auctions is very different from the reality.

> "Make no mistake: the sale, not the price, is the primary purpose of an auction."

Temptations

Two of the greatest motivating factors in human behaviour are *fear of loss* and *desire of gain*. Auction agents make liberal use of fear. The message is clear - "If you don't auction you could miss out on a really big price." They fail to state that the same price - or better - can be obtained without auction. Here is an amazingly simple point which one agent made - "*The buyers buy because they want the homes. If there were no auctions, the same buyers would still buy the same homes. And, in most cases, they would pay more.*"

This agent made another important point about low prices at auctions - "*It is hard to get the highest price from buyers by taking them to a crowded room - or out the front of a property surrounded by strangers - and yelling at them!*"

The 'Crunch'

One of the most distasteful sights in real estate is the auction 'crunch'. To see agents bully sellers to drop the price is to witness one of the most abhorrent of all sales standover tactics.

One home-owner who was considering selling at auction, attended an auction to see what happened. He described the scene:

"*Agents in black suits were circling the crowd. Suddenly, right in front of me, three men swarmed around an elderly couple. I realised this couple were the owners of the home which was being auctioned. The bidding had stopped at $341,000. The agents were urging the sellers to say 'yes'. I heard the lady say, 'We want $380,000. That's the lowest we'll go.' One agent said, 'You'll never get another chance like this. The lady said, 'You told us we'd get $400,000.' The agent said, 'The market is not telling us that. This is what the buyers are saying. They are the ones who set the prices.'*

This elderly couple were very distressed. One agent's face was just inches from the man's face. I had an urge to drag him away. I couldn't believe people could be virtually assaulted like this. The elderly man grabbed his wife's arm and then waved his other arm as if he was giving up.

Suddenly one of the agents leapt up and screamed, 'It's on the market!'. A few seconds later the auctioneer yelled, 'Sold!'.

The elderly couple stood up and an agent led them away. The agent was smiling but the sellers looked so sad. It was horrible."

The 'Stimulate' Trick

What this person witnessed was the final stages of the conditioning process, the 'crunch', together with one of the most unethical temptation tricks in real estate.

It's the trick of persuading sellers to lower the reserve and put the property "on the market". The agents tempt the sellers by saying, "If you put it on the market, this will stimulate the bidding. The price will go up." Sellers who fall for this trick discover, to their horror, that their home is usually sold immediately.

Two Reserves

Home-sellers are often told that the reserve price protects them from selling too low.

But there are two reserves. The first is the one you set when you decide to auction. The second is the one you set just before, or at, the auction, the one you have been 'conditioned' to accept. The second reserve is always below the price you thought you would get when you chose auction as your method of sale.

Deceptions

> ## "Real estate auctions are riddled with fraud."

A statement which accurately describes most real estate auctions is: *"deceit, trickery, sharp practice or breach of confidence by which it is sought to gain some unfair or dishonest advantage."* This is the Macquarie Dictionary's definition of 'fraud'. Real estate auctions are riddled with fraud.

The Quoting 'Hooks'

Sellers are hooked into auctions with the promise of a high price and buyers are hooked with the promise of a low price. But how can the sellers get a high price and, at the same time, the buyers get a low price? It is not possible.

The truth is somewhere in the middle. The sellers get less than they were told and the buyers pay more than they were told. And the agents get a commission, no matter what.

These methods of 'hooking' people are known as "over quoting" - to the sellers and "under quoting" - to the buyers.

Text-book Example

Imagine you want $300,000 for your home, but the agent believes it is worth less. If the agent tells you this, you might choose another agent. With auction, the agent can use such words as 'might' and 'maybe'. Most agents will use the 'wonder sale' trick. They will tell you about a home which sold at auction for tens of thousands of dollars extra.

So, you sign up for auction.

The agent now starts telling the buyers that your home 'may' or 'might' sell for 'around' $250,000. Or the agent will quote a 'price range' by saying '$230,000 - $270,000'. The agent will reassure you that this is the strategy to attract buyers and you should not worry.

This, on its own, should make you worry. If an agent will use a deceitful trick on buyers, the same will obviously be done to sellers.

Some agents use the expression, *"Bidding to start from"*, followed by a price of $200,000. Again, to appease you, the agent will say this is to "attract buyers".

And yes, it does attract buyers - but mostly those who can only pay around $200,000. Come the day of the auction, you may have three or four buyers who expect to buy 'from $200,000'. The agent will pressure you by saying, *"This is what the market is telling you"*.

> "...your agent is looking in the wrong market."

But your agent is looking in the *wrong* market.

You are being forced *down* in price because the price hook attracts the *wrong* buyers. Oh sure, the price goes up with an auction and sure, some of these buyers will go up from $200,000. But when the 'crunch' comes at the auction, you'll crack and sell for a lower price; most sellers do.

You can see how you lose, but how do the buyers lose?

How Buyers Lose Too

In some cases there are several buyers at an auction, all of whom want to buy for what they were *under* quoted. They have paid between $500 and $1,000 each for professional advice and inspections. These buyers lose their money.

Imagine the distress of buyers who are told they 'may' get your property for $200,000 - and they have paid for advice and inspections and have their hearts set on your home - when they get to the auction and discover the reserve price is out of their range.

When the buyers complain, the agents use this as 'proof' that auctions mean high prices. The truth is that the buyers have been duped with a low quote, just as the sellers were duped with a high quote.

Research

A survey,[6] conducted in Melbourne, revealed that eighty percent of home-sellers received a lower price at auction than quoted to them by the agent. In Brisbane, a poll of one major network's auctions showed that *100 percent of sellers received a lower price than they were quoted.*[7] In both cities, most sellers said they would never use the same agent again.

Real estate consumers can barely believe, in these times of supposed high consumer protection, that such deceptions still exist.

'Dummy' Bids

> "You are pressured into making a major decision based on false information."

Dummy bidding is the auction system's most notorious deception. Despite the denials of Institutes and their agents, most agents use dummy bidders to make fraudulent bids, (or the auctioneer will use 'phantom' bids by pointing towards walls or trees as if they are people).

Ironically, some sellers give tacit approval to this deceit because they believe it pushes the price up. But dummy bidding deceives sellers as much as buyers - usually more so.

The agents have a real challenge when there is only one genuine bidder. They need dummy bidders.

Say your lowest (reserve) price is $250,000. The agent wants to get the genuine buyer as high as possible before 'crunching' you to reduce your reserve.

If the bidding starts at $200,000, the next bid will be the dummy. Back to the genuine bidder, who then increases. And then another dummy bid. And so on - until the genuine bidder starts to weaken.

The agent then approaches you with the 'crunch' to "put it on the market". The agent says, *"Look at all these people. This is what the 'market' is telling us."*

You are pressured into making a major decision based on false information. Your home is sold thousands below the price you were 'quoted' by an agent who creates the impression that everything has been done to help you. But you have been deceived.

No Bidders

For the times when there are no genuine buyers, all the agent needs is a crowd. And then the dummy bidding again deceives sellers with a great 'conditioning' trick.

Dummy bidders will stop at a price the agent has decided - which is always well short of its value.

The agent in a masterful example of 'faking sincerity', approaches the sellers and says, *"I don't think you should sell at this price. I am sure we will be able to do better later on."*

The property is then 'passed in' at a figure well below what the sellers wanted. The shell shocked sellers have now been superbly conditioned - they have spent thousands on advertising (or even worse, they *owe* thousands), they have seen a large crowd (with no buyers) and they are ready to 'listen to reason'.

The most gullible sellers drop their price and their home sells quickly - for thousands below its real value.

The 'Date'

Auctions require an exact date and time for the sale of your home. This is a huge mistake because the time may not suit the buyers. Auctions give you about 20 minutes to make a sale, whereas normal sales give you plenty of time, which means more options and a better chance of a higher price.

The agents say that genuine buyers will always come to the auction. The facts do not support this.

Newspapers often carry reports about something as simple as the weather keeping buyers away from auctions. *"The heavy rain on the weekend has been blamed for the low attendance at recent auctions,"* is a common statement.

The buyers may have a family wedding or a holiday or an illness on the auction day. The agents don't even realise they are losing some of the best buyers who don't bother to enquire about the auction because of the date and the time.

> "The most gullible sellers drop their price..."

A dreadful example of how a set time can hurt sellers occurred when a buyer had a car accident on the way to the auction.

By the time he arrived, the property had been sold for $540,000. The reserve price was $500,000. But the buyer who had the accident was prepared to pay $560,000.

It defies belief that the success of an auction depends on what else is happening on the day of the auction.

Aside from the weather - and the personal commitments of buyers, there are a string of interruptions almost every month, which cause buyers to avoid auctions.

Melbourne's *Sunday Age* (February 14 1999), made this comment: *"The first interruptions to the auction market begin next month with the Grand Prix, followed by the Easter Holidays in April."*

In May there was the Mother's Day weekend. In June there was the Queen's birthday weekend. Things are always 'quiet' in the winter months, plus there is the budget. And then in September it's the football finals. And Father's Day. And, in 1999, a State election. Plus several school holidays during the year. Try finding a weekend where there is not *some* reason for buyers to stay away from auctions.

When Auctions 'Fail'

When a home fails to sell at auction, the agents stick a For Sale notice over the auction sign, which might as well read, 'Failed'. Most failed auction properties sell for lower prices.

The 'Clearance Rate'

Another deception with auctions is the 'clearance rate' claim. Agents will say that 90 percent of properties which go to auction are sold. When this figure is compared with normal sales, it looks very impressive - and very tempting.

But again, an obvious point is hidden - the *properties which sell at auction would still have sold if they had not been auctioned*. And they could have achieved a better result both in price and the happiness of the sellers.

'Success' to an agent, means a *sale*. It does not mean sellers are happy or they received the highest price. If agents measured the success of auctions by the satisfaction of sellers and buyers, the auction system could not exist.

Buyers Do Not Like Auctions

Agents claim that auctions attract more buyers, but this is not true. Buyers do not like auctions.

A study, conducted by the Swinburne University of Technology in Melbourne, revealed that only four percent of home buyers nominated auction as their preferred method of buying a home.[8]

Said one buyer: *"I am disgusted and outraged at the auction system. The agents that use the auction system must cost sellers thousands of dollars. Buyers hate auctions and I am not an isolated case."*[9]

> "...you are choosing a method of sale which is disliked by almost all home-buyers."

Agents often have buyers who say, *"Don't bother showing us anything for auction because we are not interested."* They *never* have buyers refusing to see homes that are not for auction.

If you choose auction, you are choosing a method of sale which is disliked by almost all home-buyers.

It cannot be stressed too often - auctions make it easier for agents to make sales because with auctions, home-sellers are more easily pressured to reduce prices.

'Auction Areas'

Be careful of the statement: *"This area is ideal for auctions."* Just because a lot of people make a mistake does not remove the mistake. Or the danger.

There is even more reason to avoid auctions if your area is rife with auctions. Genuine buyers will be attracted to your home because it is *not* for auction. Agents who do not use auctions sell more homes for more money and have happier clients, especially in 'auction areas'.

Selling Before Auction

Sellers are often discouraged from selling before the auction even if there is a good offer for the home. The agent will say, *"You might get more on the auction day."*

> "...the home sells for a lower price at the auction - often to the same buyer!"

Many sellers are offered a price before an auction and many agents encourage them to refuse it. But then the home sells for a lower price at the auction - often to the same buyer!

There are two reasons many agents discourage selling before the auction.

The first is that they have not used up all your advertising money. If you have committed to spend $10,000 over six weeks and you receive a good offer after three weeks, the agent will miss out on another three weeks of 'profile' advertising.

The second reason agents discourage selling before auction - and this applies to auctions which are held 'in-rooms' - is that it is important, to them, that there are many sales on the day of the auction.

Agents try to make sure that the first and the last properties being auctioned are sure sellers. The first sale sets the mood of the entire auction. The agents encourage the crowd to clap; everything is off to a great start.

To keep the crowd, the agents make sure that the last property being auctioned is the one with the most interest. When this home sells for more than reserve and there are lots of bidders and a big crowd, the final impression created is that auctions are a big success - big crowds, lots of bidders and high prices. As one auctioneer teaches, *"Auctions are a circus and we have to put on a good show."*[10] But there are many dangerous tricks performed at auctions.

Protecting Yourself

Each week, hundreds of home sellers all over Australia lose thousands of dollars with auctions. It is a national disgrace, particularly when it happens to people who can least afford it - the poor, the elderly or the sick.

> "It is a national disgrace..."

Real Estate Institutes, franchise networks and high profile auction agents all know what goes on and most do nothing to stop it.

A Typical Case

John and Betty had lived in the Sydney suburb of Dundas for forty years. John was an invalid pensioner with a chronic heart condition. He also suffered from high blood pressure and was in remission from cancer.

In 1999, John and Betty decided to sell their home and move to a retirement village. They did what most home-sellers do - they called a local agent.

The agent suggested auction because *"auctions go up in price"* and they could look forward to *"easily receiving $280,000"*. However, they would need to pay at least one percent of the expected selling price - $2,800 - for advertising expenses.

John and Betty did not have $2,800, but when the agent agreed to deduct the advertising costs from the sale, they signed the auction contract.

> "Under extreme pressure in front of a large crowd, John caved in."

Fast forward to the day of the auction. John and Betty are nervous because there has been a barrage of bad news. The buyers don't seem to like their home. The offers have been well below what the agent told them to expect. They have heard no mention of the $280,000 they were quoted. The agent constantly says they must be "realistic".

At the auction, the bidding began at $220,000. It went up to $252,000 - and stopped. The agent urged John and Betty to reduce the reserve. They refused. This was not what they were promised.

The agent said, *"Reduce the reserve and the bidding will be stimulated. You could still get your $280,000. It's the only hope you've got. Quick, say yes, while the buyer is still here!"*

Under extreme pressure in front of a large crowd, John caved in. Betty was horrified; it was her home too, but the agent ignored her. In what she later described as "mere seconds", the buyer offered $500 more. And the auctioneer yelled, *"Sold!"*.

They were distraught. Their home had been sold for $252,500, almost $30,000 less than the agent had promised they could "easily get".

The buyer was unable to pay the deposit on the spot and the agent asked John and Betty for more time. John refused. He became angry and ordered the agent from his property.

And then came the legal demands from the auction agent who wanted his commission plus the advertising money, an amount of almost $10,000. A hefty price for deceiving an invalid pensioner.

John and Betty's case is a typical example of what happens to thousands of home-sellers when they choose auction.

What could they have done to prevent such a dreadful experience?

The auction agent is a member of a large real estate network. He is also a member of the Real Estate Institute. He is licensed by the State Government. But this was not enough to protect John and Betty. And it is not enough to protect you.[11]

The Real Estate Institute "Guarantee"

The Real Estate Institute in New South Wales advertises: *"Deal only with a member of the Institute. Our ethics and rules of practice guarantee your protection."*

A legal opinion on the Institute's "guarantee" stated:

"In my view their advertisement is misleading. This is not a guarantee in any sense of the word. The Institute cannot even enforce conclusively its own orders. If a member does not comply, all the Institute can do is expel the member. This offers no protection at all to the public. The code itself is therefore of little help to an aggrieved member of the public and falls far short of any definition of a guarantee."

Real Estate Institutes are made up of real estate agents. John and Betty did not understand this point. They did not have the knowledge to protect themselves from unethical agents, many of whom are members of Institutes.

Knowledge and Advice

The knowledge you need to protect yourself from auction agents is simple: DO NOT AUCTION.

However, if the agent is tempting you and you feel incapable of resisting an auction, then follow this advice -

1) Insist that all verbal statements be confirmed in writing, including a commitment from the agent that you will not be liable for any costs for any reason until the agent delivers on all promises made to you.

2) Pay no money and sign no documents until you have received independent advice, preferably from a lawyer.

One lawyer commented, *"I have never had a client who has had a successful auction."*[12]

Ask the lawyer to read the relevant points from this book - some may not realise just how bad the situation can be.

3) Insist on an agent who offers you a *real* guarantee which states that if you are not happy there are no charges. Many agents will tell you this is "impossible", that there are no guarantees in life about anything. Do not hire these agents.

Let the Agent Take the Risk

Real estate consumers have little protection from the deceit of auctions. The real estate industry is perhaps the only industry where you can pay huge sums of money for a service and receive nothing. Or you can receive worse than nothing - you can lose thousands.

The closest industry to real estate auctions is gambling. And that's what real estate auctions are - a gamble with a huge risk of losing thousands.

If an agent wants you to auction, insist that the agent takes the risk, not you. Most will refuse to accept this risk, which is understandable because agents are well aware of the dangers of auctions. They don't mind you taking the risk, but they won't take the risk themselves.

The auction system is designed to sell homes with almost no regard for the welfare of home-sellers. And that's exactly what it does.

As one agent in the Sydney suburb of Balmain says to home-sellers, "We won't _do_ auctions _to_ you."

Of all the methods of selling your home, auction is by far the worst.

Don't let agents '_do_' auctions _to_ you - under any circumstances.

"...insist that the agent takes the risk, not you."

AVOIDING MISTAKES

The important points of...

AUCTIONS

1. Auction is the worst method of selling any home.

2. The reserve price is your lowest price.

3. Auctions start low. That's the only reason they go up.

4. When you hear of auctions selling 'above reserve', always wonder how much they sold <u>under</u> the Buyers' Highest Price.

5. Auctions are used to 'condition' and then 'crunch' sellers.

6. Agents over-quote to sellers and under-quote to buyers.

7. Under-quoting attracts buyers who cannot afford your home.

8. Sellers are made to pay for advertising.

9. Dummy bidding is used to deceive buyers and sellers.

10. A set date and time is inconvenient for some buyers.

11. 96 percent of buyers do not like auctions.

12. Insist that the agent takes all the risk.

13. **DO NOT AUCTION.**

Method 2. OPEN LISTING

The more agents you have, the lower the price you receive!

Open listing means you hire more than one agent to sell your home. The first agent to find a buyer at a price you accept is the agent you pay. The other agents get nothing.

The advantage with this method is that you are not committed to one agent. If your home does not sell, or if you sell it yourself, you owe nothing to anyone. With so many horror stories of unethical agents, an open listing appears an ideal solution because you can sack any agent at any time with no further obligation.

But there are two disadvantages with an open listing - and they are big ones: you are almost certain to have either a low priced sale or no sale.

Low Sale

The reason you receive a lower price with an open listing is that the agents are being paid to find a buyer before another agent finds a buyer. It's a race to get your home sold. The focus is to get *any* price and persuade you to accept it before another agent finds a buyer.

> "The focus is to get any price..."

You may say that you will only sell with the agent who brings a buyer at the highest price - which sounds good, but it doesn't happen that way.

Buyers Shop Around

Most buyers visit many agents. If they see your home in the window of more than one agent, the question they ask each agent is: *"What is the lowest price you can get for this home?"*

The asking price may be the same with each agent but all it takes to ruin your chance of the highest price is for one agent to say, *"I can get it for you for less."*

The same thing happens if you have two or three signs on your home. Aside from making your home look unwanted, having many signs encourages buyers to call all the agents. Again the buyers will look for the agent who can obtain your home at the lowest price.

This can't happen when you have just one agent because that agent is the only one who can sell your home. But the risk with having one agent is if the agent is incompetent, you are committed to using that agent. Hence the attraction of an open listing. You are free.

No Sale

With an open listing you may be free of obligation but you may also be free of buyers. You will get very lonely because most agents - and certainly the best ones - are almost certain to ignore your home unless the asking price is very low.

It is common for homes to be open listed for a year or more. The agents have forgotten them.

The best agents will refuse to consider an open listing. They know it is not the right way to sell your home and they won't do it. The best agents will never do anything which is not in the best interests of their clients (this is why some agents refuse to do auctions to you under any circumstances).

However, unlike auctions, open listings are not good for agents. And that's why most agents oppose open listings.

Guarantee

Instead of an open listing, ask for an 'exclusive listing' with a *written guarantee* that if the agent does not do what is promised, you can sack the agent without having to pay any expenses. This forces agents to honour their promises. It also provides an incentive to sell your home - they know that if they find the best buyer at the highest price possible, they will be rewarded.

An exclusive listing with a written guarantee will protect you from the danger of having a low sale or no sale. It is a safe and secure way to sell.

AVOIDING MISTAKES

The important points of...

OPEN LISTINGS

1.   You are not 'locked-in' to one agent.

2.   Agents focus on the speed of the sale, not the price.

3.   You are ignored or forgotten unless your price is low.

4.   The best agents will not accept an open listing.

5.   Choose an exclusive listing with a guarantee.

Method 3. MULTI-LIST

There are multiple dangers with multi-listing!

Multi-List has one of the best 'hooks', but it can give you one of the worst results. The 'hook' goes like this: *"The more agents you have, the more chances you have of getting a sale."*

It sounds good, but as with open listings, the more agents you have the more chances you have of getting the lowest price for your home.

Best Buyers With the Worst Agent

All buyers come into an area before they buy. They circulate among the agents.

If you Multi-List your home, you lose your right to select the agent who negotiates with the buyers for your home. Your home is shared among many agents in the area. The best buyer could end up with the worst agent - one you rejected. This means that an agent who is not a skilled negotiator could be negotiating on your behalf. And then you will not get the highest price for your home.

> "The best buyer could end up with the worst agent - one you rejected."

Skilled negotiators are unlikely to recommend Multi-List, which means that if any agent recommends Multi-List you should quickly reject that agent.

The Demise of Multi-List

Not only does Multi-List not work well for sellers, but many agents now realise that Multi-List does not work for them either. Consequently, in many areas, the Multi-List system has collapsed entirely.

The reason for the demise of Multi-List is that the better - and more hard working agents - realised that many of the lazy agents were exploiting them.

It takes more effort to find a seller than to find a buyer. The agents who find the most sellers are always the most successful. The most successful agents grew tired of having to share commission on their best listings.

Often, only the worst listings were placed in Multi-List, those the agents felt had little chance of selling. Homes which were Multi-Listed were considered to be either over-priced or almost unsaleable.

The Multi-List rules then changed and it became compulsory for all Multi-List agents to list all properties in the Multi-List system. Agents then began to make excuses to each other rather than give their good listings to their competitors.

In a memo to members, the Chairman of Multi-List in New South Wales highlighted six of the most common problems with Multi-List - all of which involved agents not wanting to share the best listings.[13]

As Multi-List imposed new rules, the most successful agents responded by resigning. Hence the fall of a system which rarely suited sellers and never suited the most successful agents.

Multi-List Areas

As home-sellers become more aware that Multi-List gets them a lower price and that choosing a skilled negotiator is far better than having dozens of agents - all of varying ability - attempting to sell their home, Multi-List will continue to decline.

You must be careful not to choose Multi-List simply because an agent says that your area is a "strong" Multi-List area.

You should be suspicious of groups of agents in the same area who all use the same system. Usually their prime aim is to help each other; it is not to help you.

And do not think - as some agents will infer - that you *have to* put your home into Multi-List. It is your home. You do not have to do anything unless you want to do it. And Multi-List is not something you should be doing if you want the highest price for your home.

Conjunctions

When two agents share a commission, it is called a 'conjunction'. Your agent deals with you, the seller, while the other agent deals with the buyers.

Naturally, the other agent has a closer relationship with the buyers than with you and may suggest that the buyers offer a lower price.

For this reason, you should never allow your agent to give a conjunction to another agent without first obtaining *written permission* from you. If other agents are denied a conjunction, the buyers will have no choice but to contact your agent. This is a very important point. Your agent is the negotiator you selected, so make sure all buyers meet your agent.

AVOIDING MISTAKES

The important points of...

MULTI-LIST

1. The best buyers can easily be with the worst agents or the agents you rejected.

2. It is better to stay with one agent.

3. Multi-List has declined because it is bad for agents as well as sellers.

4. Do not allow your agent to give a 'conjunction', without your written permission.

Method 4. PRICE RANGES

"Bait prices hook sellers more than buyers."

P rice Ranges are 'Bait' strategies which use a false low price to attract buyers.

The Price Range method comes in a variety of names - By Negotiation; Offers Above; Price Guide. They are all similar and they all undersell your home.

Say you want $300,000 for your home. The agent will suggest that your home display: 'Price Range $275,000 - $325,000'.

The agent will say that "lots of buyers" will be attracted by this lower price and then willingly pay the higher price.

Bait prices, which are supposed to hook buyers, actually hook sellers into underselling their homes.

'Price Ranges' have quickly fallen out of favour as most home-sellers are quick to realise that buyers are not so gullible as to fall for such a transparent trick.

Agents who suggest using a Price Range are not skilled negotiators. If they were, they wouldn't use such a financially damaging strategy.

Two BIG Reasons to Reject 'Bait' Prices

There are two reasons why you must never allow an agent to display bait prices for your home.

The first reason is that the *lowest price the buyers see is the highest price they will want to pay.*

> "...the person you are negotiating with should be able to afford what you are selling."

How would you feel if you saw a home advertised with the words, "Offers above $250,000". Would you offer $320,000 just because it is "above" $250,000? Of course not. You would look at the $250,000 and do what most buyers do - offer $250,000. Or less.

The second reason you must avoid bait prices is that most of the buyers you attract will only be able to afford the lowest price displayed.

If a buyer has a maximum limit of $250,000 and sees your home advertised "from $250,000" (when you want $300,000), the buyer is going to be attracted to your home. You then have a buyer who *cannot afford* to pay what your home is worth. It makes no sense unless the agent intends to talk you down in price, which is precisely why agents use 'bait' prices.

One of the principles of negotiation is that the person you are negotiating with should be able to *afford* what you are selling. If you want $300,000 for your home, the first thing you want is a buyer who can *afford* $300,000. It's such an obvious point it is amazing so many agents don't see it.

Activity Traps

Agents claim that the more buyers who are attracted to your home, the better it is for you.

But what would you prefer: dozens of buyers who can't afford to buy your home or one buyer who can?

The *quality* of the buyers is much more important than the quantity.

Agents want you to see lots of activity because it makes it easier to convince you to lower your selling price.

The agent will say, *"Look at all these people who have come through. The reason they haven't bought your home is because the price is too high."*

Or, when crowds of people who cannot afford the price you want are looking at your home, they will offer what they can afford. And then the agent will say: *"The buyers are all telling us that the most they will pay is $250,000. This is what the market is saying. You have to meet the market."*

It is the same as the Auction System - your agent is looking in the *wrong* market.

If your home is worth more than $300,000, your agent must show it to people who can afford to pay more than $300,000. This will mean less crowds and less activity. But at least you won't be under-sold.

> "You won't receive the highest price if you are attracting the lowest price buyers."

You won't receive the highest price if you are attracting the lowest price buyers. Do not fall for this activity trap.

No Price

Never market your home without a price.

When you hide the price, the buyers will hide too. Displaying no price - or using the words 'Price on Application' - makes it look as if your home is over-priced. You lose the most genuine buyers.

Research shows that when you hide the price you lose at least half the enquiry; and this could be your best enquiry. If buyers see your home *and* its price and then they enquire, these buyers are sure to be genuine.

Time and Patience

When your home first goes for sale, the right buyer may see it immediately and pay the highest price on the spot. This is great news. It is one of the best things that can happen to you.

But, if your home does not sell in the first couple of weeks, you may have to wait until your agent finds you the best buyer at the highest price.

Some home-sellers get agitated unless lots of people inspect their home. But it is better to have silence and wait for the right buyer at the highest price, than activity and sell to the wrong buyer at the lowest price.

It can take time to get the highest price for your home. That extra time - and that better agent - means you will receive the highest price possible. And that's exactly what you want.

AVOIDING MISTAKES

The important points of...

PRICE RANGES

1.   Price Ranges attract buyers who cannot afford your home.

2.   The lowest price you display will be the highest the buyers want to pay.

3.   Price Ranges force your price down.

4.   If you display no price, you lose half the best buyers.

5.   Agents who use Price Ranges are not skilled negotiators.

Method 5.
SELLING PRIVATELY

"The only reason to sell privately is to save losing money with the wrong agent."

You can save several thousand dollars in commission by selling without an agent. You can also lose several thousand dollars on the price of your home by selling it too cheaply.

If you find an agent who is a skilled negotiator and you receive a guarantee of no charges until your home is sold, you will almost always get a better price with that agent.

But if the agent is not skilled at negotiating, a private sale could be your best option.

Simple

> "You can also lose several thousand dollars..."

Selling a home the way most agents sell homes, is very simple. Agents want you to think it is complicated so that you will employ them.

What is so complicated about placing an advertisement in the paper and sitting at an open inspection and waiting for a buyer to show up? A growing number of home-sellers are finding out that selling privately is easy if they copy the typical agents.

Before you decide to sell privately, call a few agents. Unless you are convinced that you have found an agent who can do better than you, don't hire an agent. Sell your home yourself.

Three Choices

You have three choices: 1) Hire a typical agent; 2) Sell privately or 3) Hire a skilled agent.

Skilled agents get higher prices. The problem is finding one. If you can't find a skilled agent, then you have to ask yourself if it is worth paying for an unskilled one. The answer is no.

> "...the skilled agent gives you the highest net price."

Here's what may happen: 1) A typical agent may sell your home for $285,000; 2) You may sell it for $290,000 which gives you $5,000 extra on the price plus the commission you don't pay; 3) A skilled agent may sell your home for $313,500 or even more. Obviously, in this situation, the skilled agent gives you the highest net price.

These are the three prices and choices you must consider. The big difference between the best agent and the typical agent is that the best agent is 'risk free'. If this agent does not get the price you want, you pay nothing. If you can find the best agent, give this agent your home. Start with your best choice.

Private Sale Companies

Another alternative is to use a 'Private Sale' company. These companies help you with signs, advertising and some general advice. A Private Sale company charges you around a thousand dollars, which is much better than using a typical agent. However, a Private Sale company will mean paying money 'up front' with no guarantee of any result. So, again, a skilled agent who offers you 'no risk' is better than a Private Sale company.

> "The best sale you make is the hiring of the best agent."

The only reason you should consider selling your home privately is to save money. And you will save the most money if you find the best agent. Also, it is good to have a person between you and the buyer - provided, of course, that you trust that person. It is not easy when selling privately to look at a buyer and say, *"Give me more money."* It is much easier to use a third party. A good agent acts as a 'buffer' between you and the buyers. The best sale you make is the hiring of the best agent.

The answer to the question, *"Do you sell privately?"* is 'Yes' if you can't find a skilled negotiator. And 'No' if you can.

So remember, you are looking for an agent who is a skilled negotiator, a person you feel comfortable with and a person you trust to handle your valuable asset. Such agents are your best investment, both for getting the highest price for your home and for making life easier for you.

AVOIDING MISTAKES

The important points of...

SELLING PRIVATELY

1. Only sell privately if you can't find a skilled negotiator.

2. An agent is employed to do more than you can do yourself.

3. The best agents are 'risk-free'.

4. Private Sale companies require 'up-front' payments.

5. Your best investment is the best agent.

Method 6.
THE SMART SALE

"Sellers get the best price.
Buyers get the best homes.
Agents get more sales."

Selling a home is a private and personal experience, filled with emotion. As you have seen, it can also be a nerve-racking experience. But not if you have a good agent and your personal needs are the agent's priority.

The method of sale you are about to see looks after you in two ways: It gives you the highest price and the lowest stress. It is a smart way to sell because it eliminates the risk and increases the price. The Smart Sale, in legal terms, is called a Private Treaty Sale.

> ## "...everyone gets what they want."

This means that your home is offered for sale with a price for all to see. Done correctly, it is much more than just putting a price on your home and hoping it sells.

The best way to get the highest selling price is to start with a high asking price. In stages, you lower your asking price until you receive the highest selling price. It works beautifully.

This is the Smart Sale method of selling. It is open, honest and straightforward. It deceives no one. It suits sellers, it suits buyers and, when used correctly, it suits honest agents.

Everyone wins because everyone gets what they want. Sellers get the best price with no risks and no hassles. Buyers get the best home they can afford without being deceived. And, by giving sellers and buyers what they want, agents get what they want - more sales.

The most important factor to sellers is the price and the most important factor to buyers is the home. If a home suits the buyers and they can afford it, they will gladly pay the highest price.

Kerry and Sue Rowley were looking for a home in Sydney's Hills district. They found one they liked. The price was $350,000 and a 'great buy'. They were about to sign the contract, when they saw another home for $450,000 which was 'over priced'. They liked the first home but they *loved* the second home. They made their decision on emotion not price.

As Sue said, *"Paying the highest price is a small price to pay for the home we love."* Besides, their home has since increased in value by $100,000. They bought the home they wanted, paid the highest price to the owner and, after many happy years, the home has increased in value.

Sellers sell on price, but buyers buy on emotion and then price.

Attitude and Skill

Many agents lose thousands of dollars for home-sellers simply because they have the wrong attitude towards price. If they think a home is over-priced they will ask buyers to make an offer, which of course, encourages a lower price.

The best agents rarely ask for an offer. *They ask buyers if they want to buy.*

If you see a home for sale and ask a typical agent - *"What's the lowest price I can get it for?"* - you will often be given a lower price. This reckless attitude toward price is rampant in real estate offices where poorly trained salespeople cost sellers thousands almost every time they speak.

Compare the difference between a skilled agent (Agent A) - who understands negotiation - and a typical (incompetent) agent (Agent B). Say the asking price of a home is $500,000.

Buyer: *"What's the lowest price I can get it for?"*

Agent A: *"$500,000. Is it what you are looking for?"*

Agent B: *"They knocked back an offer of $450,000 last week. They might listen to $460,000."*

If the buyers can afford $500,000 and they love the home, Agent B has just lost $40,000 for the sellers!

Skilled negotiators aren't scared of price. They focus on what the buyers want to buy and what the buyers can afford to buy. Selling for the highest price has two stages: First, finding a buyer who wants your home, and second, obtaining the highest price the buyer can afford to pay.

With the Smart Sale method, the price is out in the open, which removes one of the greatest sales killers - fear and suspicion.

Risk and Trust

The 'Smart Sale' method is also a safe method. You are under no obligation to pay any fees until your home is sold and you are happy. The agent takes the risk, not you. If you do not sell, you lose nothing.

Trust

> "The agent takes the risk, not you."

An iron-clad rule when selling is never to hire an agent you don't trust. Trust is the major ingredient in any relationship - business or personal.

The best agents win trust when they take risks away from home-sellers. They ask nothing from you until they produce a result you are happy with. Nothing that is, except your trust.

So, if there is no risk and you are confident you will get the highest price possible, allow the agent to get on with the job of finding the right buyer. You have nothing to lose and everything to gain. It's the smartest way to sell.

Price Dangers and Truths

There are two dangers to avoid when deciding on the asking price of your home. The first is 'too high for too long' and the second is 'too low for too many'.

If the price of your home is too high, it could attract no interest. If you leave it too high for too long, buyers may wonder what is wrong with it.

If your price is too low you attract too many buyers in the wrong price range.

Instead of giving you false hopes and 'conditioning' you later, the best agents will clearly explain the best strategy to get you the highest price.

> "You cannot ask for more than the highest price..."

But remember that the *highest* price could be lower than the price you want. And that's the truth. You cannot ask for more than the highest price, regardless of how this price compares with what you want.

Let's say you want $500,000 for your home.

The worst agents suggest an auction saying you can get more than $500,000. But, as you have seen, by the time of the auction you will have been 'conditioned down' to the point where $450,000 will look wonderful. And *that's* the deception.

Asking Price and Selling Price

Asking Price and Selling Price are often two different prices. The way to get the highest *selling* price is to start with a high *asking* price. Do not be ashamed of your asking price. Be proud of it. Confidence is very important.

Starting high is one of the most important points in negotiation. You then lower the asking price until one buyer says,

'Yes'. This is the *only* way you can be certain of getting the highest price in any market. It is the opposite to an auction where you begin with a low price, climb up and stop below the highest price.

To illustrate the strength of the Smart Sale strategy, let's continue to say you want $500,000 for your home.

> "Do not be ashamed of your asking price.
>
> Be proud of it."

If you have followed the advice from Chapter One, you will have obtained a valuation from an independent valuer *before* you put your home for sale.

Let's say the valuation is $475,000.

But, let's also say an agent told you that you could get "well over $500,000" at auction. Although you may realise that this is a bait to 'hook' you, it is still tempting. You may think, *"What if there is a buyer who will pay more than $500,000? I don't want to miss that chance."*

You won't.

The Price Mountain

Whatever you might get with auction, you will get more with this strategy, as you will see with the Price Mountain example.

The mountain is triangular (like a pyramid). Imagine there are **prices** on this mountain.

At the very peak you see $560,000. You know this price is highly unlikely. As you come down the mountain, the prices descend in $10,000 lots. At the bottom is $400,000. You know that $400,000 is ridiculous. Your home would never sell so low.

However, at auction, the bidding would "start from around $400,000". An auction agent would be baiting buyers who could afford *"around the low to mid four's"* (as they call it). Come auction day, all you have are buyers who can't afford to pay anywhere near the value of your home (this is exactly how thousands of sellers are duped with auctions). You can forget the $500,000 you wanted. Your climb *up* the Price Mountain is set to halt at $450,000 - maybe a little bit more, if you are lucky. That "well over $500,000" bait, is slowly fading.

Now, watch how the Smart Sale method takes care of you by making sure the price you get is the *highest possible price*.

Price Levels

On the Price Mountain, there are three major Price Levels - the Top, the Middle and the Bottom. Each level has a 'range'.

The range for the Top starts at $560,000 and goes to $500,000. The Middle goes from $499,000 to $450,000 and the Bottom goes from $449,000 to $400,000.

Now, picture **people** on the mountain. These people represent genuine buyers.

The Bottom Level is crowded with buyers, all ready and able to pay $400,000 for your home. This is the Bargain-give-away-price. And you are not interested in this price.

> "...you would have no chance of getting the highest price at auction..."

As you go up the mountain, the crowd dwindles. At the Middle Level there may be two or three buyers who can pay between $450,000 and $475,000. You are getting close to the valuation price. Above this level it becomes cloudy. You can't see if anyone is on the mountain.

The Top Level - from $500,000 to $560,000 is completely obscured. You don't think there is anyone up there. But you can't be sure. So you put a question mark on those clouds. The question mark means, *"Is there a buyer above $475,000?"*. If so, where is the buyer and *what* price will that buyer pay? Is the buyer at $490,000 or $500,000, or maybe even $510,000? Could there be a buyer even higher than this?

PRICE RANGE

$560,000
$550,000
$540,000
$530,000
$520,000
$510,000
$500,000
$490,000
$480,000
$470,000
$460,000
$450,000
$440,000
$430,000
$420,000
$410,000
$400,000

The Price Mountain

Stay away from lots of buyers at the base of the mountain.
You want one buyer - the one who's highest on the Price Mountain.
Start at the top and come down. It's easier and safer.

If there is *one* buyer who can pay $540,000 and the next highest buyer can pay $475,000, you would have *no chance of getting the highest price at auction* because you are climbing *up* the mountain. When you get to $475,000, the buyer who can pay $540,000 will make one more bid of a thousand dollars (maybe $5,000). This means the most you will get is $480,000. The agent would call this a "success".

And you would be another 'hidden victim' having sold your home for $60,000 less than the buyer was prepared to pay.

For Buy Price

You have to know what the buyer is prepared to pay. Remember, it's called BHP which means Buyer's Highest Price.

The only way to know what a buyer can afford is to *know* the buyer. This is where the Smart Sale method beats any other method. It insists that all buyers are qualified so that the agent can know the Buyers' Highest Price.

If a buyer thinks, "*I will buy this home for $540,000*", the agent must know this price. It is also called the **'For Buy Price'**. It is the most important information to make sure you get the right 'For Sale' price.

The 'For Buy' price can only be found by starting at the TOP of the mountain - or just below the summit. Picture the agent walking down the mountain looking for buyers. This is easy compared with starting at the bottom.

> "The only way to know what a buyer can afford is to know the buyer."

This is how you get the highest price for your home. Most agents don't understand this simple negotiating point, and this is why most home-sellers lose thousands of dollars.

Here is the truth. Your home is worth somewhere around $475,000 - that's what the unbiased valuer told you. You want $500,000. With a 'Smart Sale', you would have received $540,000 for your home. With an auction you would have received $480,000 which would have put you $60,000 out of pocket.

There is only one possible choice if you want the highest price - don't auction, use the Smart Sale method. Start with a high asking price and then come down until you get the highest selling price.

Several Asking Prices

Before your home is sold, there may be several 'Asking Prices'. The first asking price will be the highest. When no buyer is found, you go to the next highest asking price - the next level down the mountain. Keep going down the mountain until a buyer is found. And then decide if you will accept the highest price.

Finding the Highest Buyer

The first thing the agent will do is look for a buyer who is already in the area. All buyer 'contacts' will be scanned looking for buyers who have two ingredients - they can afford to pay "around $500,000" and the home matches what they want.

A sign will be placed on the property. This will alert buyers looking around the specific area. The agent will also do what most agents never do - make personal contact with people who live close to the home to ask if they know of anyone who may want to buy. (Many buyers live in the local area).

The agent needs to be careful not to lose any buyers who may be shocked at the high asking price. This is where the skill of the agent is critical. No reasonable buyers should be ignored. For instance, if a buyer says, "*$540,000 is far too much. I wouldn't pay more than $500,000.*" In a few weeks, that could be the highest paying buyer. The agent will keep in close contact with this buyer.

The agent will always be truthful and the truth is that the sellers want to sell their home for the highest price. The agent will say to any interested buyer - *"If the price you can pay for this home is higher than any other buyer, then I will speak with the owners and see what they say."*

If there is no interest at $540,000, the agent will go to the next level and see if there is any interest. And so on, until the highest buyer is found.

The Three Outcomes

When your home first goes for sale, or each time you adjust the 'Asking Price', there are usually only one of three things which happen.

First, you may have no interest and no offers. This means the asking price is too high.

Second, you may get lots of interest and no offers. Again, this indicates the asking price is too high or there is something inside the home which the buyers dislike.

And third, you may have lots of interest and lots of offers, in which case, you focus on the buyer who makes the best offer.

> "...focus on the buyer who makes the best offer."

Unique and Special Homes

The Smart Sale method works brilliantly with very expensive homes, the ones that some agents refer to as *"ideal auction properties"*. (There is *no such thing* as an ideal auction property.)

As one agent, from South Yarra in Victoria, said: *"Auctions are costing millionaires millions. The more valuable your home, the more you lose if you auction."*

The Hedges Avenue Example

> "...at an
> auction
> each buyer
> knows
> how much
> the other
> buyers
> are offering."

Hedges Avenue on Queensland's Gold Coast is one of the most desired addresses in Australia. Beautiful homes lead straight onto the beach. The agents say, *"This is the ideal street for auctions. It has all the right 'auction ingredients' - uniqueness, scarcity, prestige, wealth and desirability."*

When an older style home came up for sale, the agents urged auction, saying that anything else was "financially suicidal" (a common 'baiting' lure for auctions).

The auction agents told the owner that he may get "a million or more" at auction, although privately they said the home was only worth about $850,000, or maybe $950,000, if the bidding went high enough. They wanted at least $10,000 for advertising.

But one agent explained the 'Smart Sale' method. The seller said he had never looked at it in such an obvious manner. Because he had nothing to lose and everything to gain, the seller chose the 'Smart Sale' method.

The home was listed at an asking price of $1.2m dollars. As expected, there was lots of interest. The calls poured in from buyers all wanting to know: *"How much?"*

When they heard the asking price, most buyers said, *"Far too much."* Some said, *"What will he take?"*. This is where the skilled negotiator shines. The reply to the "How much will they take question" is always, *"They will take the asking price... How much will you pay?"*

One of the *perceived* advantages of auction is that "competition" among buyers gets a higher price. But there is a major flaw in this 'perceived' advantage - at an auction, *each buyer knows how much the other buyers are offering.* Instead of offering their highest price, all the buyers do is offer a little bit more than the buyer they are competing with. This keeps the price as low as possible. It does not take it to the highest the buyers will pay.

The agent found three buyers who would pay more than $900,000 and then spoke privately with them all and asked: *"What is the most you will pay for this home?"*

Buyer 1 said, $900,000.

Buyer 2 said, $950,000 and...

Buyer 3 said, $1,050,000 dollars.

The agent then said to each buyer. *"There are two other buyers who are very keen. I am asking each buyer to tell me their highest price. The owner will sell to the buyer who pays the most. Is your price the most you are prepared to pay?*

Two of the buyers asked how much the other buyers were offering. The agent refused to say because this would have meant that each buyer would then offer just a little bit more than the next buyer, instead of offering their highest price.

Skilled negotiators understand this point - and they use it.

The agent gave the buyers time to 'think it over'. The next day he called them again.

Buyer 1 said $900,000 was her highest price. She would not pay more.

Buyer 2 increased his offer from $950,000 to $1 million and said "not a cent more".

And Buyer 3 said he would pay $1.11 million - an increase of $60,000.

The agent now had three offers from three buyers and all the offers were the highest each buyer could pay. He had the BHP for all three buyers! This is something an auction can not do.

> "The owner will sell to the buyer who pays the most. Is your price the most you are prepared to pay?"

The home was sold to Buyer 3 for $1.11 million; exactly $110,000 more than Buyer 2's final offer.

At an auction, here's what would have happened:

Buyer 1 would have stopped bidding at $900,000. Buyer 2 would have stopped at $1m dollars and then Buyer 3 would have bid another $10,000 and bought the home for $1.01 million - $100,000 below his highest price. *$100,000 would have been lost with an auction.*

This destruction of other people's money is common in real estate. And most people don't even realise what is happening to them.

With the Smart Sale method you *always* get the highest possible price. You can count on it.

AVOIDING MISTAKES

The important points of...

THE SMART SALE

1. This is a Private Treaty sale. And with a skilled negotiator as your agent, it is the smartest possible way to sell.

2. Start with a high Asking Price and lower in stages until you receive the Highest Selling Price.

3. There is no risk for the seller. All risk is with the agent.

4. You may have several Asking Prices at different stages.

5. There are three outcomes at every Asking Price level.

6. The Smart Sale is ideal for unique and special homes too.

7. You always get the Highest Price.

Chapter Eight

PRESENTATION

"You rarely need to
spend thousands of dollars
to make your home attractive."

Falling in Love

◆

First Impressions

◆

The Outside Appearance

◆

The Inside Atmosphere

◆

The Value of Major Improvements

◆

Exclude ALL Inclusions

◆

Focus on Features

◆

**Your Competition
in the 'Market'**

◆

Finding Positives

Buyers are attracted by the appearance of your home and, when they inspect it, they are influenced by its atmosphere. The right appearance outside, followed by the right mood inside, gives you the best chance of getting the highest price.

You rarely need to spend thousands of dollars in renovations or repairs to make your home attractive. All you have to do is pay attention to some obvious points, all of which can make a big difference to your price.

Falling in Love

Buying a home is emotional. The *feeling* of a home is more important than its price. If your agent has 'qualified' the buyers, they will not be 'lookers', they will be genuine people who can afford your asking price. Their feelings will be the main reason they accept or reject your home.

The word 'love' is common with home-buying. Buyers say, *"We loved that home and that's why we bought it."* So, make sure you present your home at its finest. Remove or fix anything which might 'turn off' the buyers.

First Impressions

We are attracted to homes the same way we are attracted to people. The first thing we notice is the outside. If it is clean and neat and friendly, we feel good and we want to know more. If it is scruffy or dirty, our minds seem to shut down, we are 'turned off' and we lose interest, not caring if we ever see that home again.

Buyers often say they *"just want to look from the outside"*, they want to see if they are 'attracted' by the appearance. This is how 'open inspections' lose buyers. Some homes may not look very attractive from the outside, but inside they have a real atmosphere to them (the same applies to people). If the home is open for inspection and the buyers don't like the outside appearance, they drive off, never to return.

To make your home looks its best, 'attention to detail' is crucial. When you live in a home, you overlook its little faults. It is now time to have a fresh look.

Stand in the street and look at your home as if you were seeing it for the first time. Try hard to pick faults. It is better that you find the faults while there is time to fix them, rather than the buyers find the faults. Try to judge your home by the standards buyers will use, not by your standards. See it through their eyes.

The challenge is to make your home as attractive as possible without spending too much money.

The Outside Appearance

> "Flowers do wonders for the front of a home,..."

First impressions create permanent opinions, so create a positive mood with a positive first presentation.

Begin by sweeping the front street. Remove all rubbish from the gutters. Clear the letterbox of junk-mail. If you have a lawn, make sure it is not bone-dry. Green grass is appealing and a sprinkler does wonders to most lawns. Water always creates a fresh and clean appearance.

If you have a gate make sure it doesn't squeak. If your front fence needs repair, it might be better to demolish it. If the buyers see a potential expense, they either won't buy or they will expect a reduction in your price.

Hose the paths and the outside of your home to remove dust and cobwebs (close your windows first). And clean the windows so that they sparkle; few things are as ugly as dirty windows.

Make sure there is no paint-flaking. You may not have to re-paint, but at least scrape off any loose paint pieces. And clean the gutters of leaves.

Flowers do wonders for the front of a home, and the brighter the better. They create a homely look. You can get flowers for any season. Daffodils, pansies, petunias - go to your local nursery and ask for advice.

Buy flowers in pots if you don't have much lawn and make sure they are displayed in two places: near the street and near your front door.

> "Create an appeal which says, 'Welcome. Come inside'."

You want buyers to fall in love with your home, so give your home that loved look.

At the front door, have a thick door-mat with 'welcome' on it. It sounds corny, but it *feels* good. It is friendly, it feels like home.

Make sure that the screen door is working. Have a door-knocker or a bell with pleasant chimes. If you have a door bell, make sure it works. The sound of a door bell with a flat battery is *not* a feel-good sound. If people come to your home in the evening, have the welcome light on.

When buyers arrive, you want them to think, *"This looks nice"*. By the time they reach your front door, you want them to think, *"This feels nice. I like it."*

Neat, clean and friendly are the first steps to making your home attractive from the outside. Create an appeal which says, *"Welcome. Come inside"*.

The Inside Atmosphere

Inside, your home should *feel* like a home. It has to be warm and appealing. One agent described it by saying, "A *home should look and feel 'happily lived-in'*".

Natural

Make the atmosphere natural and relaxed, even if it means changing (or *improving*) your living habits. Buyers are aware of gimmicks such as a coffee pot brewing, a cake in the oven or classical music playing softly in the background. False attempts to add appeal often have the reverse affect.

Genuine appeal is what wins the buyers. A radio or a TV - never too loud - is a natural part of home life. Well-made beds with warm quilts, lots of pillows and the ultimate mood enhancer - the teddy bear, really make a home feel like home. Home truly is 'where the heart is' and anything which increases the emotional feeling of comfort is something we all love.

> "False attempts to add appeal often have the reverse affect."

Nothing turns people off more than bad smells, so be sure your home is fresh. You can buy plug-in fragrances which remove bad odours. If you have pets, be careful because their smell, while familiar to you, can be unpleasant to others. Take the pet bowls outside. A dog which jumps up can be irritating and distracting (but not as bad as a savage dog which bites the buyers). The rule is *remove your dog*. Take it for a walk.

Make sure the home is bright and airy by opening the curtains. Fresh air, if practical, is always best. If you have a fireplace and it is winter, an open log fire can be a big selling feature. At the very least, make sure your home is warm in winter and cool in summer.

Try to remove clutter from your home so that it does not look smaller than it really is. The time for a clean-up or a 'garage sale' is *before* you sell, not afterwards.

Most homes have some natural untidiness - a book beside the bed, a newspaper in the kitchen or slippers on a floor - this is acceptable and expected. What is not acceptable is dirt.

Make sure the bathrooms are clean to the point of sparkling. Fresh fluffy towels add a warm feeling as does the sound of a washing machine or the sight of clothes blowing in the breeze on the outside hoist. Atmosphere is everything.

The bathrooms and kitchen are especially important to a woman who is usually the major decision maker.

Minor Repairs

If there is any unfinished work in your home - such as skirting boards which have been removed - fix these things. If there are any obvious minor repairs - such as door handles missing or broken hooks - fix those too. Repair all irritating things which are likely to catch the eyes of buyers.

> "The best advice is to do all you can to make your home feel like a home."

Be very careful if you do any painting. Painting one dull room can suddenly make other unpainted rooms look dull too. Before you know it, you could have a major painting job on your hands. This could lead to replacing the carpets and even the tiles in the bathroom. Suddenly you are involved in a very expensive renovation.

The cleanliness and the mood is most important, but all expense needs careful consideration. Will you get your expenses back? Ask your agent's opinion.

The best advice is to do all you can to make your home feel like a home. Make it sparkle without making it too immaculate or clinical. Some sellers create a show-home. In doing so, they create a cold sterile effect.

Homes with warmth are the most attractive and appealing.

During the Inspection

When an agent is showing your home it is best if you (and your dog) are not home. Too many people in a home make it look small (this happens at open inspections if hoards of 'lookers' are squeezing past each other).

If you must stay at home, do not remain in the most appealing room. Buyers will be conscious of their intrusion into your life; they rarely feel relaxed when you are in the same room. Genuine buyers take their time to inspect a home so make sure they have this time.

If you trust the agent, let the agent stay with the buyers. And don't expect the agent to point out all the obvious features. Some of the best salespeople are silent when buyers are inspecting a home. The time for most questions is *after* the inspection or if they require a second or third inspection.

The Value of Major Improvements

If you spend enough money you can always make it easier to find a buyer, but this makes no sense if the cost of the improvements are too high. It would be better to reduce the asking price.

Most major improvements are personal and do not add the value you expect. An example is a swimming pool. If you pay $30,000 for a pool, the pool salesperson may tell you this will increase the value of your home. But if the buyers don't want a pool you will not get back what you paid.

Most home improvements often return only *half* their cost upon sale. You may have to wait years to find a buyer with the same personal taste as you.

If your home needs major renovation, it may be better to avoid the expense of renovation and have a lower asking price. Many buyers want to renovate a home to suit their own taste.

Minor improvements can give you a great return on your selling price, but major improvements are often a big mistake. Either spend a little bit of money to sell your home or spend a lot of money and don't sell.

Exclude ALL Inclusions!

Here is a presentation idea that will increase your chance of receiving the highest price.

Always offer your home for sale without major inclusions.

There are two types of inclusions: the *basic* inclusions and the *major* inclusions. Basic inclusions are carpets, curtains and standard light-fittings. Major inclusions are dishwashers, micro-waves, security systems, special light-fittings, pool equipment, custom furnishings and anything else which you may be tempted to include to help 'make' a sale.

If, in your eagerness to please, you have included a host of extras, you will have nothing left with which to bargain, other than money.

It works like this: The buyers inspect your home and see the magnificent inclusions which cost you several thousand dollars. If they are interested in buying, they will ask, *"What stays with the home?"*

But your answer has no effect on the buyers' decision. They were going to buy anyway, no matter what you said. If you say, *"Nothing stays,"* or, *"Speak with the agent who knows all those details,"* you will have an excellent way of negotiating later when the buyers make you an offer.

Let's say you are asking $500,000 and you are selling your home without the major inclusions (which have cost you $50,000). If the buyers offer you $450,000, you can use the inclusions to prevent you from lowering the price too much. Your agent can say, *"Look, they will not reduce the price, but they may consider leaving some inclusions worth several thousand dollars."*

There are two things to remember: Firstly, no-one will buy your home just because you are offering 'extra' inclusions. The area, the atmosphere and the price are far more important. Secondly, no matter what price you are asking, most buyers will make you a lower offer.

In their eagerness to make their home 'more' attractive, most home-sellers make the mistake of giving away too much too soon.

A rule of negotiation is to *never offer something you don't have to offer*. Save the major inclusions for later and you will save thousands of dollars.

Focus on Features

Your home's features are its biggest selling point. The price is secondary. Sure, if there are two identical properties, then the price is important. But most homes are unique and each has a special 'feel' which makes it more or less attractive than other homes. Even an apartment in a building of look-alikes can sell for a higher price if the owners give it that special touch.

This is why it is so important to focus on the features of your home. What are the best features of your home? Other than price, *why* should someone buy it? Make a list of these features and make sure buyers are told about them.

Selling a home can be cruel. You may hear that your home is too small or too big or too old or too new or that it needs too much work. You will hear negative features you never considered, so it is vital that you fight these negatives with a list of positives.

When people focus too much on the price of a home they tend to forget its features. And this means you may have to reduce the price or the buyers will choose a similar home at a cheaper price.

Almost all buyers make their decision based upon the features of a home. It could be something as simple as a tree on the front lawn. Buyers buy homes they love first, and homes they can afford second. Features are more important than price. Focus on features.

Your Competition in the 'Market'

Any market involves competition and your competition comes from two places: other homes for sale and other agents. The presentation of your home and the skill of the agent can mean thousands of dollars to you in the real estate market.

> "Your home has to be a better 'product'..."

Your agent has to persuade buyers to inspect your home and to buy it in preference to other homes. Buyers have a choice - your home or someone else's. Agents have a choice - sell your home or sell someone else's.

Agents can 'switch' buyers from one home to another fairly easily by saying something positive or negative about either home. This is just competition in the market. It is the same as Honda 'switching' a buyer from Holden by stating the positives of a Honda and the negatives of a Holden. Holden may do the same, in reverse. Competition is part of a free-trade market. It inspires companies to offer a better product. Your home has to be a better 'product' and you have to have a better agent than other sellers.

Finding Positives

Many negatives are actually positives when viewed in a different way. For instance, a small block of land is often a negative, but it can be a positive for people with ill-health. It can also be a positive for a business couple who do not have time for gardening. Look for the positives in any negatives. They always exist.

Your agent should sell the positives of your home, and when necessary, sell the negatives of homes with other agents. This does not mean your agent should mislead people. It means that your agent works for you and not for the other home-sellers or their agents.

An Up-Market agent

Sometimes it can pay to choose an agent in a neighbouring but slightly more expensive suburb. The reason is simple: The buyers in the more expensive suburb will have been looking at higher priced homes. Many will consider buying a better home at a lower price in a nearby suburb. If your home is offered for sale alongside more expensive homes, it has more appeal than if offered for sale among cheaper homes.

Contact

Make sure your agent is easy to contact. Many agents spend thousands of dollars in advertising and then allow their phones to go unanswered in the evenings. If a buyer wants to find an agent after hours, the agent who is easy to contact is the one the buyers find.

Your Reason

Be sure your reason for selling is confidential. No-one, other than the agent you trust, should know why you want to sell. If the buyers know you have a pressing reason for selling, this could be used against you.

It is enough for buyers to know only that you *want to sell*. The *reason* is your business. Revealing it could weaken your position when you receive an offer.

The best agents will tell you how to give your home that special feeling which wins the hearts of buyers.

With the right agent and with your home looking its best, you will always get the highest price.

AVOIDING MISTAKES

The important points of...

PRESENTATION

1. The feeling of your home is more important than the price.

2. Make your home attractive without spending a lot of money.

3. First impressions create permanent opinions, so make sure the outside makes the buyers want to come inside.

4. Your home should look and feel natural. Cleanliness is more important than tidiness.

5. Avoid using the 'transparent' presentation tricks.

6. Attend to all minor repairs.

7. Do not count on major improvements to increase the price by the cost of the improvements.

8. Exclude all inclusions. This is a great negotiating aid.

9. Focus on the positive features of your home.

10. Never publicly reveal your reason for selling.

Chapter Nine

OPEN INSPECTIONS

"It is amazing - a person needs
more identification to hire a video
than to wander through
a family home!"

Dangerous

◆

Restrictive, Inconvenient
Impersonal and Frustrating

Opening your home for public inspection is one of the worst mistakes you can make. It is always a financial mistake, but it can also be your worst emotional mistake.

Dangerous

Do you ever leave your front door open and allow strangers to wander through your home? Of course not. It would be madness. Anyone might come through.

This is *exactly* what happens when your agent holds your home open for inspection. Anyone is invited to just march up to your front door and wander through your home. They walk through your lounge room, they go into your bedrooms and they open cupboards. Total strangers intruding into the heart of your personal world. This is very dangerous.

> "Total strangers intruding into the heart of your personal world."

Your local video store will not rent a $10 movie without identification, yet all over Australia, anyone can walk into any family home and agents barely notice. Agents will even tell complete strangers how alarm systems operate.

Just because your home is for sale, it doesn't mean you have to place your safety at risk. It is your home. You have a right to know who enters it.

When selling, the only people who should inspect your home are people who are likely to buy it. You want buyers, not burglars. And the only way to know if a person is a buyer or a burglar is to identify them *before* they enter your home. It is very hard to do this with a sign on the street saying "Open For Inspection".

Do not underestimate how serious this is. Neighbourhood Watch advise,[1] "When your home is open for inspection, your valuables, are also open for inspection."

Ask at your local Police Station or ask your insurance company. They know the dangers, that is why your home is usually not insured when open for inspection.

Cover-Ups

> "Your home is usually not insured when open for inspection."

As with most systems which hurt sellers and help agents, the dangers are publicly 'played down' by the real estate industry.

In Queensland, the Real Estate Institute said the dangers posed by Open Inspections is only a "minor problem[2]". Try telling that to the people whose homes have been burgled. Try telling that to the broadcaster, Derryn Hinch, who lost personal items worth an estimated fifty thousand dollars when thieves visited his agent's open inspection.[3]

Robbery keeps Hinch a headliner

Derryn Hinch

DISCERNING thieves have stolen furniture valued at up to $50,000 from Derryn Hinch.

They took the antiques from the five-bedroom house at the broadcaster's Mt Macedon vineyard, sold yesterday for $805,000.

Hinch believes the thieves returned on Tuesday or Wednes-day after spotting the furniture during a real estate inspection.

Gone is a 19th century com-mode belonging to his former wife, actor Jackie Weaver, a writ-ing desk and a Wellington chest.

Kyneton police are investigat-ing.

Hinch, 54, completed his move from Melbourne to Adelaide with the sale of 11ha Brookfarm, which produces wine for the Macedon Ridge label.

Hinch plans a future on the Internet. He is setting up Hinch-Web Radio to broadcast a weekly current affairs show and conduct chatroom sessions.

– DEREK BALLANTINE

In Victoria, the Real Estate Institute issued a confidential notice to agents saying: *"An open for inspection necessarily involves a risk that a person posing as a prospective purchaser may come into the house and steal items."*[4]

The Institute recommends a letter be sent to home-sellers which says, *"…we cannot be on the spot to detect every incidence of theft."* It advises agents to tell home-sellers to remove *"anything attractive to a thief."*

The Institute suggests that two salespeople attend an open inspection. For larger homes, it is recommended that *"more agents are in attendance to keep the property safe"*.

In Western Australia, the Institute issued a warning to agents about thefts during open for inspections.[5]

In South Australia, as early as 1991, the Real Estate Institute, after discussions with the Police Department, told agents to *"make it clear that liability for any loss or damage at an open inspection falls upon the home-seller."*[6]

It also stated that a security guard be at all homes which are open for inspection. Neighbourhood Watch goes further - it recommends that sellers have a friend in *every* room of their home while it is open for inspection.

After the Inspection

The biggest point which agents - and most home-sellers - ignore, is the danger *after* inspections. Some agents say they have been doing open inspections for years and they have "never had a problem." These agents miss a fairly obvious point: your home will rarely be robbed *during* the open inspection. Thieves do not load your possessions into a van while the open inspection is taking place. *They come back later.*

Mr and Mrs Elkington are social workers who are well aware of the dangers from their work with criminals. They wrote: *"Open inspections provide chances to 'case the joint' for a later return. Violent criminals admit to us that they learn house layouts from open inspections and have subsequently broken in with plans to rob and/or sexually assault the occupants."*[7]

A police officer described harrowing accounts of people finding their homes ransacked in the weeks after open inspections.

He said, *"From a woman's perspective, a burglary is a terrifying experience regardless of the fact that she is not home at the time. The sight of her personal items being violated only escalates the terror."*[8]

This police officer is appalled that most agents have no idea of the consequences of open inspections.

One of the worst cases occurred in the Sydney suburb of Eastwood.[9] During an open inspection, a window was unlatched. The criminal returned a few nights later to kidnap a child.

Qualifying

> "They will sort 'prospects' from 'suspects'."

There are two questions to ask before anyone comes into your home: *'Who are you?'* and *'What do you want?'* It is better to be blunt now than sorry later.

The best agents will qualify all buyers on your behalf. They will sort 'prospects' from 'suspects'. The best agents will respect your privacy and your safety. This is the way it should be.

Restrictive, Inconvenient, Impersonal and Frustrating

Open inspections restrict the chances of a sale and greatly reduce the chance of obtaining the best price.

If you are a home-buyer, what would you rather do - meet an estate agent who shows you homes at a time convenient for you, OR, would you prefer to drive around inspecting open-houses at a time set by the agent?

Home-buyers prefer to meet helpful agents. They are fed up with agents who do not return calls, who tell them to "inspect at certain hours" and who have a couldn't-care-less attitude.

Make it Easy to Buy

One of the Golden Rules of selling anything is: Make it easy for people to buy.

Open inspections make it hard to buy. If the open inspection lasts for one hour, that hour has to suit the buyers. If they have something else to do they cannot inspect the home. The sellers lose the buyers.

> **"Open inspections make it hard to buy."**

Michael and Lesley Johnston visited a home which was open for inspection in East Melbourne.

The agent's first words were, *"You'll have to be quick, I am about to leave."*

Michael said, *"But what happens if we want to buy it?"*

The reply was, *"Well, you'll have to meet me at the next home. Or you can come back next week, but come earlier."*

This is a common attitude of agents at open inspections.

Instead of restricting an inspection time to an hour once or

167

twice a week, a home should be available to inspect at any time to suit a genuine buyer. This is what the best agents do.

Some agents claim that open inspections are more convenient for sellers, but if sellers knew how many buyers were being lost because of open inspections they would never accept this claim.

Lower Prices

Open inspections force buyers to look at other homes which are in competition with your home. If your home is similar to others in your area (and this is particularly true with home units) and you allow an open inspection, you are going to be offered a price on par with the *lowest* price being asked by the sellers of a similar property.

Also, the buyers can make negative comments within earshot of other buyers. One buyer who dislikes your home can influence other buyers.

Buyers love the convenience of seeing properties at a time which suits them. Sellers love the prices they obtain when they avoid open inspections. Both are happy. The agents are happy too because they sell more homes, which normally happens when they do what is best for sellers and buyers.

Do not have anything to do with open inspections.

AVOIDING MISTAKES

The important points of...

OPEN INSPECTIONS

1. Open inspections are an open invitation for criminals.

2. Only genuine home-buyers should inspect your home.

3. Open inspections are inconvenient for genuine buyers.

4. Open inspections can lower the price of your home.

5. Open inspections suit agents, not sellers and buyers.

6. Never allow your home to be open for public inspection.

Chapter Ten

ADVERTISING
& MARKETING

"Millions of dollars
are squandered
on unnecessary advertising."

The Truth

◆

Behind the Scenes

◆

Kickbacks

◆

Smart Marketing

◆

Solutions

◆

Visible Activity

◆

Attracting Buyers

Real Estate Advertising is one of the best examples of the incompetence and dishonesty in the real estate industry.

Home-sellers are being duped into spending millions of dollars on unnecessary real estate advertising through a system known as Vendor Pays Advertising. (VPA).

Since the introduction of this system, real estate advertising has reached record levels. There is now approximately twenty times as much advertising being done, yet there is no noticeable increase in the number of sales being made. In fact, in most areas, the number of home sales is declining.

Agents have taken to advertising with great enthusiasm since sellers began to foot the bill.

Whatever you do, do not fall for the mistake of handing over thousands of dollars to an agent for advertising.

This chapter will tell you how to avoid one of the worst mistakes made by home-sellers today.

The Golden Rule of Real Estate Advertising is: **You do not need to spend huge amounts of money on advertising to sell your family home.**

The Truth

There are three reasons agents advertise. The first is to promote themselves. The second is to impress each other. And the third is to influence home-sellers.

Agents state that advertising attracts buyers. But at what cost and at whose cost?

The cost is enormous. And most of it is a total waste of money. The agents won't tell you this, of course. But behind the scenes, they all know the real purpose of advertising, as evidenced by these words from the Real Estate Institute of New South Wales:

"Ads are not written to sell the advertised property. Only 6 percent of ads lead to the successful sale of the particular property (according to one source).[1] *Sellers might be alarmed to learn that the advertising they are paying for has a slim chance of selling their property."*

Promote Agents

The main reason for advertising is not to promote your home. It is to promote the agent.

The biggest part of all real estate advertisements is the name of the agency. Agents want to make themselves 'look good'. They call this 'profile' which is a big word in real estate.

A statement from a course held by the Real Estate Institute of Victoria, says, *"The more ads you have with your name on them, the more successful you will look."*[2]

Impress Each Other

The 'success' of a real estate agency is commonly measured by the size, number and frequency of its advertisements. There are awards for agents with the most advertisements. Hundreds of faxes are sent from the head offices of networks urging salespeople in branch offices to do more advertising and beat the other networks. *"We must raise our profile"*, is the constant message.

There are gala dinners with prizes for salespeople who have persuaded home-sellers to pay the largest sums of money for advertisements.

In New South Wales, the Real Estate Institute has an annual dinner sponsored by *The Sydney Morning Herald*. In a glittering night of ceremony, a string of awards are presented to agents based on their "image" and "marketing campaigns". The prizes are trophies plus free advertising space to the agents.

One angry home owner who lost $7,000 on advertising her home, which failed to sell, asked this question: *"Why do Real Estate Institutes have awards for advertising and not for client satisfaction?"*[3]

She could have been speaking for hundreds of sellers who lose thousands of dollars every week.

Attract Buyers?

Agents rarely advertise to attract buyers. The buyers are already *in* the area.

Think about it. What is the one thing all home-buyers do before they buy in an area? *They come into the area.* They choose the area and then they choose the home.

Take the advertisements away and the buyers won't disappear. Homes would still be sold because buyers would do what they have always done - visit an area before they buy.

Granted, advertising brings *some* buyers to an area. But, again, the questions must be asked: *At what cost* and *at whose cost?*

Let Agents Pay

If the agents want to advertise, let them pay for it. *"It's too expensive"*, will be the reply.

The reason advertising is too expensive is because agents do too much of it. This is not the fault of home-sellers. It is the fault of the agents. No home-seller should have to pay for mistakes made by incompetent agents.

Impress Home-Sellers

Agents often carry copies of their advertisements to impress you, in the hope that you will perceive them to be successful. *"The perception is the reality"*, is a phrase often heard in real estate. But the perception is *not* the reality. The perception is the *deception.* Don't let yourself be deceived by the 'look' of a real estate agent. You need to look behind the look. Be suspicious of any agent with a large number of advertisements. Just ask yourself: *"Who is paying for these advertisements?"* And make sure *you* don't pay for them.

Behind the Scenes

One of the greatest scandals in real estate involves agents who take money from dozens of sellers in the *same* area for advertising which attracts the *same* buyers.

Seller A pays an agent $5,000 and Seller B pays the same agent $5,000. And so do Sellers C to Z! The same buyers then come to each property. But each home-seller pays.

Home-sellers often pay thousands to an agent and get nothing in return because this money is paid regardless of whether their home sells or not and regardless of the price for which it sells.

> "The advertising cost per home could soon average $10,000 in some areas."

The Multi-Million Dollar Spend

The biggest 25 agents - in terms of *spending* - who advertise in *The Melbourne Age* spend more than $20 million a year of home-sellers' money.[4] This is almost a million dollars per agency - for just one newspaper.

This is in addition to what they spend in other suburban newspapers. The advertising cost per home could soon average $10,000 in some areas. All over Australia, sellers are being ripped-off with advertising expenses.

A World of Ego-Mania

One 'high profile' agent, in Melbourne, boasted during a lunch that he had been given $14,000 by a home-seller while he was aware of a definite buyer for her home.

"Why would you want to take the money if you already have the buyer?" asked another agent. The boasting agent looked puzzled as he answered, *"Profile mate. We all know what this business is about."*[5]

What is particularly disturbing about this story is that this agent later became the President of the Real Estate Institute of Victoria. When asked about it, his reported response was, *"Yes, sure I said that. But we all do it."*

Protecting Yourself from Advertising Rip-Offs

The only way to protect yourself from being ripped off with advertising expenses is: *never pay any money to any agent until your home is sold.*

If enquiries to protect consumers can be conducted into other industries, why is the real estate industry being ignored?[6] Perhaps it is because most home-owners only become home-sellers once every ten years - even longer. Collectively, they are losing thousands of dollars a day. But, individually, they are only losing thousands every ten years.

Many home-sellers do not *realise* they are losing thousands. They do not know what goes on 'behind the scenes' at the lunch tables and in the real estate classrooms.

People who investigate corporate crime will confirm, *"The worst cons of all are those where the victims do not realise they are being conned."*

> "If enquiries to protect consumers can be conducted into other industries, why is the real estate industry being ignored?"

These 'profile' agents will argue that they are not doing anything illegal. However, being legal does not necessarily mean being ethical.

Kickbacks

Another unethical practice is advertising 'rebates'.

Rebates - or 'kickbacks' - involve agents being paid a commission by newspapers on advertising money taken from home- sellers. These kickbacks are up to forty percent of the money paid by home-sellers to advertise their homes. This gives agents a bigger percentage for selling advertising than for selling real estate.

> "Many agents take hundreds of thousands of dollars each year in kickbacks which their clients, the home-sellers, are unaware of."

It works like this: A home-seller pays five thousand dollars to an agent supposedly to cover advertising costs. The newspaper provides an account so that the agent can justify that the money has been spent on advertising. But, behind the scenes, the newspaper pays the agent up to two thousand dollars. This is the kickback.

Kickbacks are one of the big reasons advertising costs have exploded in the last twenty years.

Many agents take hundreds of thousands of dollars each year in kickbacks which their clients, the home-sellers, are unaware of. This conduct, while technically legal, is highly unethical.

In Victoria, legislation is pending to make kickbacks illegal with penalties of up to five years imprisonment for guilty agents.

Home-sellers should avoid agents who take kickbacks.

Smart Marketing

Agents talk about the need to "market" a home. But when most agents say 'marketing' they mean 'advertising'. Advertising is just a small part of marketing, but it can soon become the most financially dangerous part.

Identify the Customers

One of the basic principles of marketing is to *identify your customers* and find them in the most economical manner.

Al Ries and Jack Trout are world authorities on marketing. They say, *"More money is wasted by business reaching out to non-customers than by anything else."*

If there are two ways of finding the buyer for your home, and one way costs $5,000 and the other way costs $500, surely you would choose the cheapest way. This is what 'smart marketing' is all about. It's about *not spending money that you don't have to spend.*

Wasting Millions to Reach Millions

When your home is advertised in a major newspaper, you may reach a million "readers", but all *readers are not home-buyers.*

Only one and a half percent of the population are in the market to buy a home at any one time. This means that there are 15,000 home-buyers for every million newspaper "readers".[8]

Now comes an important marketing question: How many of these 15,000 buyers are interested in your suburb?

On average, it works out to be about 25 buyers per suburb. These are your only customers. No one else matters.[9]

Let's ask another simple question. Of these 25 buyers, how many would already be looking in your suburb? The truth is all of them.

Sure, research from the newspapers may tell you that "80 percent of home-buyers read the paper." But what they don't tell

179

you is that *100 percent of home-buyers visit your area before they buy.* They also don't tell you that you are paying to reach a million readers you don't need to reach!

> "...all readers are not home-buyers."

If you have something which suits a million people - such as Corn Flakes - then use the major newspapers and get value for every dollar you spend.

But you are not a multi-national corporation. You are a home-seller with a home-seller's budget, being influenced by people who use your money to promote themselves.

Incompetence or Dishonesty

It is obvious that most real estate agents have never studied the most basic principles of marketing.

To convince sellers to spend their money on advertising, one Melbourne agent uses the statement: *"You can't keep it a secret."* This enables him to take hundreds of thousands of dollars from home-sellers to promote himself. (This is in addition to his kickbacks.)

Smart marketing does not mean paying thousands of dollars to tell 'non-buyers' about your home. Agents who make such mistakes on behalf of sellers can only be either incompetent or dishonest.

The Real Cost of Advertising

Many agents, once they study marketing, are horrified at what they have been doing with their clients' money. These agents then stop advertising in the major papers and save themselves and their clients thousands of dollars each month.

There is one 'smart marketing' point which really shocks agents who study marketing. The point is made with a series of simple questions.

Question: *"How many sales did your agency make last year?"*

Answer: *"180."*

Question: *"How much money was spent on newspaper advertising?"*

Answer: *"$495,000."*

Question: *"What is the average advertising cost per house?"*

Answer: *"$2,750."*

Now, here comes the grand slam question:

"How many of the 180 buyers bought their home solely because of newspaper advertisements?"

The answer is always similar to what the Real Estate Institutes already know - *about six percent of sales come from newspaper advertising.*

If an agent spends $495,000 on newspaper advertising and makes 11 sales as a direct result of that expense, this means that the cost to sell each of the 11 homes is $45,000!

One agent explained it well: *"Newspapers reach lots of people. All buyers are people but not all people are buyers. Agents who advertise outside their local area are crazy. But, we all know the reason they advertise in the big papers is not to get buyers, it's to increase their profile."*

Cost Versus Return

The only intelligent way to gauge any result is to look at the return from the expense.

Dan Kennedy, author of "Ultimate Marketing"[10] *says, "The worst marketers get to their grade-A prospects only by lucky accident; by throwing out their message to everybody and letting the right people find it. This is like getting a message to your Aunt in Pittsburgh by dropping 100,000 copies of your letter out of an airplane as you fly over Pennsylvania. I call this 'blind archery.' Blindfolded, given an unlimited supply of arrows and some degree of luck, you'll hit the target eventually. And you will hit it once out of every x times you shoot an arrow. Of course you'll also hit innocent bystanders, bushes, fence posts, stray animals and everything else around. And arrows are one thing. Dollars are another. Nobody has an unlimited supply of dollars to play with."*

> "Demand an agent who will use skill, effort and intelligence to market your home."

Kennedy is referring to companies that spend their own money. One of the most often heard statements in real estate is: *"The advertisements cost me nothing. The sellers pay for them."* Agents who make such statements believe they have an unlimited supply of dollars - your dollars. Don't let them use your money to build their profiles. Demand an agent who will use skill, effort and intelligence to market your home.

Teaching Agents

The Real Estate Institute in New South Wales advertised a course - *"How to get Vendor-Paid Advertising."* It said, *"the extra money you make will pay for the cost of the course."*[11] This means that the money paid by home-sellers, ostensibly for advertising, is going to the agents to pay for the Institute course.

This is the same Institute that said home-sellers would be "alarmed" if they knew what happens to their money.

Home-sellers should be even more alarmed at an Institute which admits that advertising is ineffective and then teaches agents how to get home-sellers to pay for it.

Solutions

The agent you choose has to do two things for you: Find the right buyer for your home and persuade that right buyer to pay the most they can afford.

Your agent has to be a good marketer and a good negotiator. Add honesty and you have an agent who could be ideal for you.

The 'Open' Agent is the Best Agent

Most buyers 'shop around' in an area, looking at homes and making contact with agents. Your agent should be easy for buyers to contact. Agencies should be open seven days with extended trading hours until at least 7pm. Their phones should be answered at all times - day and night. This makes it easy for buyers to contact them.

Courtesy

Agents should also be approachable. They should treat buyers with courtesy. You want an agent who spends time qualifying buyers.

One top selling salesperson, from the Gold Coast in Queensland, said, *"It always amazes me that agents always know the price of the homes they have for sale, but they rarely know the prices the buyers will pay."*

Another agent, in Melbourne is constantly selling homes for better prices than other agents. She puts it down to one reason - *"I know what my buyers will pay."*

While the other agents are spending time with dozens of 'lookers' at open inspections, this agent is spending time with a few genuine buyers. *"Too many agents waste too much time. That's why they make so few sales. They are always busy doing nothing."* This agent is very popular with buyers because she does something her competitors don't do - she takes a genuine interest in finding them what they want.

Smart marketing is finding the right buyer and this means being easy to contact and then being prepared to spend time with the right buyer.

Buyer Records

Most agents get dozens of calls from buyers each week. Some get hundreds. The best agents keep detailed records of all buyers who contact them.

> "The best agents keep detailed records of all buyers..."

But most agents keep no records. Some tell the buyers to watch their advertisements and call if they see something. And then they ask sellers to pay for advertising so they can find a buyer! Insist on an agent who keeps records of buyers and who follows up buyers.

Local Buyers

The closer someone lives to your home, the higher the price they are likely to pay. One of the first things the best agents do is approach people who live within five hundred metres of your home. So often agents spend a fortune on advertising only to find that the buyer lived nearby.

One terrible example happened in the Sydney suburb of Mosman. A home-seller spent $50,000 on newspaper advertising only to have the home sell to a buyer who drove past and saw the For Sale sign.

One agent commented, *"Yes, but it was a very expensive home."* This is typical of the attitude shown to home-sellers in expensive areas - "it's OK to waste their money. They've got plenty."

You should always market your home in your local area. The best buyers - meaning those who pay the most - often enquire to the agent from a For Sale sign.

Visible Activity

Marketing involves qualifying and negotiating, two of the greatest sales skills. These are skills that get you the best price. But often, these skills are silent skills. You don't see a lot of activity.

It can be easy to think - when you don't see your property being advertised or you are not holding open inspections - that your agent is doing nothing. You could be tempted to say, *"All the other agents seem to be doing something. What are you doing? I want some action."*

If you trust the agent - and you are not paying anything until your home is sold - do not demand advertising or more inspections.

> "The best agents get the best price and they do it with effort you may never see."

The best agents always bring the lowest number of people to your home. They rarely disturb you. The reason is simple. Only one buyer can buy your home and the best agents always look for that one buyer. They are not sitting at your home with flags flying and handing out floor plans and brochures to neighbours and 'sticky beaks'.

The reason for much of the visible agent activity in real estate is to make you *think* there is *"lots happening"* and to persuade you that the agent is doing lots of work. If the price has to be reduced, the agent can point to all the visible activity and say, *"Look at what we have been doing."*

It is not important that you see the agent, but it *is* important that the right buyers see the agent.

Be careful demanding visible activity. The best agents get the best price and they do it with effort you may never see. If you ever want to know what your agent is doing for you, visit their office in the early evening - between six and seven - and you'll see the real action.

Attracting the Right Buyers

The first purpose of real estate advertising should be to attract all buyers to the office. It does not mean advertising all homes listed by the agency because this will attract the same buyers and increase costs. It is more important that the agent attracts every *buyer rather* than advertise every home. Then the agent will bring the most suitable buyers to your home.

Sorting Buyers

Once the buyers contact the office, they are sorted by their requirements. This is the qualifying stage.

The agent then matches each buyer with homes which may be suitable. It is simple, it saves time and it delights the buyers to have an agent who listens to them.

It's one of the biggest marketing points in real estate: *buyers who want to buy in an area always come into the area before they buy.* This statement should be mounted on the wall of every real estate office.

The Buyers' Road

The best agents use a *"buyer attracting strategy"*, described by one agent this way: *"We look at our area as if it is an ancient town. All buyers who want to buy in our town must come down one road. When they get to the town gates, we ask a question - 'Are you coming here to buy a house?' Those who say 'Yes', we speak with. The others we wave on with a smile. Meanwhile, the other agents are running all over the countryside - in other towns and villages looking for buyers."* It's a nice analogy which explains why this agent, from southern Victoria, has quadrupled his agency's sales since he switched to 'smart marketing' three years ago.

Information

Too many agents give too much information too early about homes for sale. Not only does this show a lack of marketing skill, it shows a lack of negotiation skill.

One of the principles of negotiation is that you should never tell too much too soon. If an advertisement is packed with information there is no need for the buyer to contact the agent. And no contact means no sale. The purpose of any form of marketing is to attract enquiries, not to do the selling.

For Sale signs, which attract the most genuine of all enquiry, are a prime example of how some agents have no idea about smart marketing.

> "The purpose of any form of marketing is to attract enquiries, not to do the selling."

In addition to the words, "For Sale," some agents write many details on the sign. And here's what happens. Instead of receiving a phone call and having an opportunity to speak with the buyers, the buyers make a decision from the information on the sign. The agent loses the contact.

Too Much Information

The more a genuine buyer talks with your agent, the more chance the agent has of selling your home. But many agents rely too much on sales aids and gimmicks to do the selling for them. Sellers are paying an agent to SELL their homes, not to rely on brochures or floor plans to do the selling.

Here's how you could lose a sale by allowing the brochures to do the selling: If the buyers are wondering about the size of your rooms and they have a floor plan, they don't need to speak to the agent. If the rooms are too small, the floor plan can't talk to them. It can't say, *"They might be small rooms but aren't you forgetting the large built in wardrobes?"*

Talking Signs and Windows

Some agents have 'talking signs'. The sign displays an FM radio frequency which the buyers, outside the home, tune in to and hear a detailed description of the home.

Other agents have 'talking windows', where the buyers stand outside the real estate office and look at photos in the window and push buttons. A loud-speaker gives them information about the home. If they are interested they can talk into a little microphone and leave their details.

What ever happened to *"Hello. How may I help you?"* One of the most pleasant experiences for any customer is to speak with a human.

Be wary of any agent who relies too much on technology for giving out information. Ask agents what they know about marketing and negotiation, not technology.

Simplicity

Real estate marketing is very simple. Don't let any agent convince you otherwise. Marketing means finding the right buyer - without spending more dollars than is necessary. This is Smart Marketing.

Once the buyer is found, that buyer must be qualified. If there is a chance that the buyer may be interested in your home, the agent will arrange an inspection.

With the right agent, you will soon have the best buyer at the best price, without wasting thousands of dollars on unnecessary advertising.

AVOIDING MISTAKES

The important points of...

ADVERTISING AND MARKETING

1. Agents advertise to promote themselves, not your home.

2. Very few homes are sold from advertising in major newspapers.

3. Despite twenty times as much advertising, the same - or less - number of homes are being sold.

4. Many agents receive huge kickbacks from newspapers.

5. Advertising reaches millions of readers but most readers are not home-buyers in your suburb.

6. As all buyers come into an area before they buy, agents should focus on their local area.

7. If agents had to spend their own money on advertising, they would spend far less.

8. Never pay money in advance to an agent for advertising.

Chapter Eleven

TROUBLE-SHOOTING

"Your greatest protection
is an honest, highly skilled
and hard-working agent."

WHAT TO DO...

If You Have Chosen Auction

◆

If You Have Paid Money in Advance

◆

If You Have Signed a Harsh Agreement

◆

If You Have Allowed Open Inspections

◆

If You Are Being Threatened

◆

If You Have Chosen Open or Multi-List

◆

If You Are Being Ignored

◆

If You Receive an Offer

◆

If Your Home is Not Selling

◆

If You Decide Not to Sell

◆

If Strangers Come 'Knocking'

◆

If You Want to Complain

I f your home is already for sale, you may feel upset about mistakes you have already made. But, provided you have not sold, it may be possible to save yourself from further harm. If you *have* sold, then, except in the most extreme cases of financial loss, there is probably little you can do other than be wiser next time.

If You Have Chosen Auction

Call the agent and cancel the auction. Confirm this in writing by sending the letter in the Appendix of this book.

Make it clear that cancelling the auction does not mean cancelling the sale. Tell the agent to speak with all genuine buyers and let them know that you are keen to sell, but not by auction.

The agent will try to talk you out of your decision. You will be told that there are many buyers and they will be competing with each other at the auction. If this is true, the buyers can compete with each other now - there is no need for an auction.

Ask if the agent knows the highest price each buyer can pay. If the agent does not know this, ask why. Tell the agent that you expect this information to be known.

Do not allow the agent to bully or intimidate you. It is your home. The agent must follow your instructions.

Use the negotiating technique known as the 'broken record' - repeat your decision no matter how much pressure is applied to you. Just keep saying, *"Our decision is final. We do not want a sale by auction."* If the agent persists, say you have read this book and you are aware how auctions cost home-sellers thousands of dollars by selling below the buyers highest price. You can say that the agent should have known this. *"Why didn't you tell me?"* is a powerful statement to transfer the pressure back to the agent.

Make sure that the auction sign is removed and replaced with a new For Sale sign.

If your agent says *"Auctions are best in this area"*, tell the agent to give you the names of the last ten people who sold by auction and the last ten people who bought at auction with that agency. Make sure it is the most recent ten and not ten that the agent selects.

Call the ten sellers and ask them if they were pleased with the agent and then call the ten buyers and ask them if they were pleased with the price and *how much more they would have paid*. These 20 calls will show you how close you came to losing thousands at an auction.

If You Have Paid Money in Advance

Ask for an immediate refund. Insist that no more of your money be spent promoting the agency. Tell the agent that you are now aware that money spent on advertising is more for the benefit of the agent than for your benefit.

If the agent argues, quote the sections from this book which say that the Real Estate Institutes claim that *"advertising is to make the agency look good,"* and that *"most ads do not sell the home advertised."* Ask why the largest part of the advertisement is the name of the agent. Suggest, strongly, that at the very least, the agent should pay for the cost of advertising the name of the agency.

Tell the agent that you are aware that some agents charge zero commission just to have the advertising money from home-sellers to promote their agency. Some agents will even pay the home-sellers a fee if the advertising money is large enough. [An agent in Sydney's Hunters Hill paid a home-seller $3,000 and charged no commission just to have the $40,000 to advertise the home - which was really to advertise the agency.]

If you are being asked to pay thousands for advertising, at least insist that you are charged no commission when a sale happens.

If You Signed a Harsh Agreement

Read carefully through your agreement. Make sure you understand what you have signed. Just because it is copyright to the Real Estate Institute, does not mean it is in your best interests.

Look for any clause which concerns a kickback. It will be called a 'rebate' or a 'volume discount' and it will state what the agent is 'entitled to' and what the agent will 'receive' and what you 'agree' to. Ask the agent if there is a kickback paid on your money. And then say, *"Did you intend to keep this money or were you going to pass it on to me?"*

Look to see how long you are committed to the agent and what rights you have if the agent does not do what was promised to you. Most real estate listing agreements have no consumer warranties.

If you feel you have been misled, say so. If an agent has given you a high quote and is now attempting to talk you down in price, you are the victim of misleading conduct. You should not meekly accept such treatment. You should be outraged. Tell the agent that you wish to cancel the listing agreement. Use the letter in the Appendix of this book. (Appendix Letter 4)

If You Have Allowed Open Inspections

Cancel all open inspections on your home. Tell the agent that the only people who are permitted to enter your home are genuine buyers who have been identified by the agent. Insist that the agent accompany all buyers to your home.

The agent may deny that there are security problems with open inspections, but point out that the danger is not *during* the open inspection, it is afterwards when the agent has gone.

Check with your insurance company to make sure you are covered for any thefts that occur as a result of past 'open for inspections'. For the next few weeks be very careful to keep watch over your home. If you feel uncomfortable, arrange to have your locks changed.

Tell the agent that one of the main reasons for holding an 'open for inspection' is so the agent can generate 'leads' for other home-sellers in the area. You do not want to be used as a source of leads for the agent.

If You Are Being Threatened

Stand up for yourself. If the agent says you must pay advertising accounts or that you will have to pay two commissions if you go to another agent, threaten your own legal action on the grounds that you have been misled.

And then seek legal advice. All lawyers are aware of the ethics of many agents and will write a strong letter to an agent for a modest fee. A letter mentioning legal action for misrepresentation will be enough to make most unethical agents take notice. Ask your lawyer what the total costs are likely to be if you have to fight the case. Compare the cost against the demands of the agent. Be guided by your lawyer.

If You Have Chosen Open or Multi-List

With an **open listing**, contact all the agents and tell them you want to select one as your exclusive agent. Ask each agent: *"What can you do to get me the highest possible price for my home if you are my exclusive agent?"*

Select an agent you feel comfortable with and who you believe is the most competent. Do not make the mistake of wanting to be 'loyal' to one agent because you might socialise together. You need the *best* agent.

Ask for a written guarantee. Do not sign agreements with any agent for more than six weeks unless you receive a written guarantee that you can cancel the agreement if the agent does not fulfil the promises made to you.

With **Multi-List**, contact the agent with whom you signed the agreement and ask to be released from the agreement. Tell the agent that you only want the agent of your choice to speak with potential buyers of your home. If you are comfortable with the agent, ask that the Multi-List agreement be replaced with an exclusive listing agreement. Again, be careful with the time period.

If You Are Being Ignored

As hard as it might be, try to remain calm if you complain. And avoid being rude, no matter how upset you feel. Ask simple questions such as, *"Why are you ignoring me?"* or *"Do you feel your agency is giving me good service?"*.

Tell the agent clearly, what you expect. For example, if you want to be notified after every inspection on your home, say: *"I'd like you to tell me what the buyers are saying about my home. Can you do this for me?"*. If the agent says, "Yes", then say, *"I will be pleased to keep you as my agent if you will attend to this for me."* It's a positive comment but the message is there - you are ready to dismiss the agent if you are not satisfied.

In extreme cases, *call other agents*. Few things upset an agent more than losing business to another agent. You will instantly go from being ignored to being important.

> "Many agents are very quick to claim their legal rights but very slow to live up to their moral responsibilities."

The Institutes have rules which forbid agents from criticising other agents. They also have disciplinary tribunals which impose fines on agents for attempting to 'solicit' the customers of other agents. (There is no allowance for whether or not the clients are happy with the agent.) This is why some agents will be reluctant to speak with you when you are 'locked-in' with another agent.

Make it clear to both agents - the one you listed with and the one you call - that you are demanding the right to fire an agent who ignores you and hire another one.

As a last resort, remove the agent's sign and write a letter saying you do not wish to sell with that agent. Collect your keys and any paperwork belonging to you.

Be careful - if you give your home to another agent while you still have an agreement with your first agent, the first agent could try to claim commission if your home is sold.

Many agents are very quick to claim their legal rights but very slow to live up to their moral responsibilities. A lawyer may tell you that if you appoint an agent on the basis of promises made by that agent and the agent fails to fulfil those promises, the agreement with the agent may be invalid.

If You Receive An Offer

If You Trust the Agent

If you trust the agent and there are three factors present, you should accept the offer.

1. The offer is the highest price this buyer can (or will) pay.

2. The offer gives you enough money to achieve what you want to achieve.

3. The offer is the highest you are likely to receive for quite some time.

The best agents will never under-sell your home. If they recommend that you accept an offer you can be assured that this offer is the highest available at the moment.

You can gamble that you may receive a better offer later. But be careful, because many sellers reject an offer and never get a better offer. On the contrary, they get lower offers and wish they had accepted the earlier offer.

The first thing to consider is what you can do with the money. Is it enough to enable you to do what you want to do? This can lead to the question of whether you should be selling at all - assuming the offer is the highest you are likely to receive.

When your home first goes for sale, the interest and the offers are likely to be at their highest. It is easy to make a mistake because your confidence is high. But as more time passes, the more your confidence drops and the more you may wish you had said 'yes' to an early offer. This is where an agent you trust is so important. Ask your agent.

The Quick Sale

The best agents keep in contact with genuine buyers which means they often sell your home quickly. Their speed might shock you.

Quick sales can mean two things: Either the price is too low or the agent is very competent. Be careful not to think the price is too low; the first buyer could be the right buyer at the right time. It could also be the only buyer for a long time.

So, if the price is right and you trust the agent, take the quick sale. Be pleased to pay an agent for being competent.

If Your Agent Lacks Skill

If your agent is not a skilled negotiator, an offer is the point where you could lose thousands of dollars. You have to be very careful.

Many agents approach a home-seller with a "great" offer. They will urge that it be accepted; they will say the buyers will "never pay more." But when the sellers reject the offer, the buyers usually offer more! This makes the sellers realise that this agent cannot be trusted to negotiate on their behalf.

Does the agent know the highest price the buyers can afford to pay? If not, why not? Say to the agent, *"If I reduce the price will you reduce your commission?"* If the agent says 'Yes' the agent is a poor negotiator. This means the buyers will probably pay more.

Paid Money?

Have the buyers signed a contract and paid money? If not, do not discuss your price. Serious buyers will pay money and sign a contract when they make an offer.

If you agree to an offer and the buyer has not paid money or signed a contract, the buyer can say "No, thanks" and suddenly you have weakened your position. The next buyer will know what you are prepared to accept. This happens when auctions fail. The buyers know the maximum price offered and it weakens your bargaining power.

If the buyers love your home and they can afford to pay your current asking price, the offer may be a 'try-on' which means if you reject it, they will still buy. How do you know what to do? Do you take the risk? In most cases, the answer is 'yes', hold out for more. Typical agents spend too much time trying to get the sellers down in price instead of trying to get the buyers up in price.

Tell the agent to ask the buyers to increase the offer. Do not say whether you will come down in price. Just say, *"They will have to do a lot better than that."* If the agent says, *"How much better?"*, tell the agent to discover the maximum the buyers can afford to pay. And then you will 'think it over'.

Inclusions

If you have offered your home for sale without 'inclusions' your agent can use these as incentives to increase the buyers' offer. It is better to use inclusions as a bargaining tool before you consider lowering the price of the home.

But, before you sign, **check with your lawyer, if you do not trust the agent.**

A Little Bit More

And finally, when you are tempted to say 'Yes', tell the agent to obtain just a 'little bit more' and *then* you will agree. Even if it is just a thousand dollars, remember this is your last chance. Once you sell, you can never get more for your home.

Agents who have studied negotiation will know several ways to have an offer increased. Has the agent asked the buyers how long they intend to own your home? If you have been offered $20,000 below your asking price and the buyers intend to live in your home for ten years, that's only $2,000 per year if they pay the full price. It's $170 per month or about $6 per day or fifty cents an hour.

This makes the buyers focus on the long term instead of the short term.

Ask the agent what has been done to increase the offer. Are you impressed with what the agent tells you or do you feel you are being pressured? Follow your instincts - that inner voice is often your best friend. Listen to it.

If Your Home is Not Selling

If your home has not sold within six weeks of placing it for sale, it either means the price is too high or the agent is no good.

The easiest choice is to blame the agent.

But the agents do not leave your home unsold because they don't *want* to sell it. They either can't sell it or they can't bring themselves to tell you *why* they can't sell it. It is hard to face you with the truth - *"Your property is too high and my skills are too low."*

You think the agent is no good and the agent thinks your price is too high. And the agent dives into the real estate 'bag of tricks' and comes up with *activity* which creates the impression of competence - auctions, more open inspections, more advertising campaigns, more brochures and the Internet. It's all designed to find something else to blame other than the price or the agent.

During this activity the agent can say, *"We tried this but it didn't work."* And then come the low offers with all the corny statements, *"This is what the market is saying." "The buyers are all indicating that your home is worth less."* The market and the buyers are to blame. You cave in, sell for a lower price and the agent gets paid.

Don't 'cave in'. Look at the likely reasons for the low offers and see how you can sell for the highest price.

The Agency

Is the agency open seven days? Do they sell many homes in the area? Does the agent possess high negotiation skills? Do you like and trust the agent?

> "...buyers buy with their hearts, but their hearts are connected to their wallets."

If you answer 'Yes' to <u>all</u> these questions, then *the reason your home is not selling is because the asking price is too high.* Lower it to an amount the agent recommends. You don't have to sell until a buyer is found. But to get more interest you often have to *move your asking price into a different level.*

Sure, buyers buy with their hearts, but their hearts are connected to their wallets. And if your home is outside their price range, genuine buyers may never see it.

You are not Lowering the Selling Price

Do not think that lowering the asking price means lowering the *selling* price, because when you have no sale and no interest, you have nothing.

The best way to sell for the highest price is to *start with a high asking price and then lower your asking price until a buyer says* 'Yes' AND to make sure that your agent is competent. Does this apply to you?

Time and Price Must Match

There is no such thing as 'no buyers' for a home. You can have a buyer tomorrow if the price is low enough. For every price there is a time attached to it. It may take years to get the asking price and it may take hours to find a bargain hunter.

You can pick a time or you can pick a price, but - and this is the big point - *the time must match the price*. The highest price for your home usually comes within the first six weeks of having it for sale. The longer it takes from that point on, the less you may have to sell it for later. So, if you are serious about selling for the highest price, do not hesitate to *lower the asking price*.

Beware of 'The Lemon Tag'

Asking too high a price for too long a time, can give you too low a price. Your home could acquire the 'lemon' tag. Buyers will begin to wonder why it is not selling. It will be almost as bad as a failed auction - these homes seem to be stamped with the word 'unwanted'.

Another Agent?

If your agent is competent, don't make the mistake of thinking you should try another agent. The same buyers circulate in the area. If you have the best agent, you can do no more than wait or lower the asking price.

When your home is not selling as quickly as you would like, other agents may contact you.

They begin by politely asking if your home is sold. And then they feign surprise because your home seems so nice and it *"should have sold."* They will pretend to be puzzled with the lack of advertising or open inspections. They will say they have many buyers who could be interested (you are supposed to believe that all these buyers do not drive around your

> "If you have the best agent, you can do no more than wait or lower the asking price."

area and see your home or your agent's signs). They will say your home *seems* to be reasonably priced.

Be warned: agents who come knocking when your home is not selling are the most dishonest agents. Ask them to give you all their comments in writing including a guarantee that if what they claim is incorrect you will be charged nothing. And then show their comments to your existing agent.

Three Choices

If you have the best agent and your home is not selling, you have three choices - lower the asking price, wait for a buyer to appear or withdraw your home from sale.

If You Decide Not to Sell

If you change your mind and decide not to sell, notify your agent immediately. First by a phone call and then by letter.

This is when you will be thankful for a 'no charges until sold' agreement. If the agency has made an effort and you are pleased, assure them that you will consider using them again one day. The best agents will understand. They will be polite. They will thank you for choosing them and they will wish you well.

The Nasty Agent

Some agents turn nasty if you decide not to sell. You will be shocked at their attitudes of 'how could you do this after all the work I have done for you'. They will play the guilt card on behalf of themselves or any buyer they are working with. Again, do not be bullied. You have the right to change your mind.

Sometimes the agent will demand payment for advertising money and attempt to take legal action against you if you do not pay their advertising accounts. You should protest strongly. However you have to consider if it is worth the time and effort to fight. One thing you can be sure of - if the agent turns nasty and threatens to sue you, that agent will never be hired by you again.

If Strangers Come 'Knocking'

Do not discuss the sale of your home with strangers and do not let anyone come through your home who knocks on your door. Not only is this for the personal safety of you and your family, it is also for your financial safety.

Some strangers suggest you wait until the agreement with the agent expires and sell to them and save commission. But who saves the commission? You or them? Some buyers are very good negotiators. They know cheaper prices are easier to obtain without the agent.

Tell the buyers that you have an agent and you will only deal through the agent. If the buyers are genuine, they will go to the agent.

Cutting Out the Agent

Sometimes your agent may show your home to buyers who will return later and ask you to sell without your agent. These buyers are placing you in a very dangerous position. If you sell to them, you will still have to pay the agent. It is the real estate equivalent of 'shop-lifting'. No matter what you think about your agent, nothing can ever justify a dishonest act. Send all buyers back to the agent.

> "It is the real estate equivalent of 'shop-lifting'."

If You Want to Complain

If you are being misled, or you have been cheated by an agent, you should complain. But to whom? A good lawyer is your best option. Lawyers handle many complaints against agents. Most wish their clients had spoken with them earlier, before the agent was hired.

> "Do not accept unacceptable behaviour."

No matter how hopeless you feel, do not ignore bad treatment. Do not accept unacceptable behaviour. Too many home-sellers do nothing because they want to put the experience out of their minds and get on with their lives. *"No more agents for a long time."*

But if an agent has misled you, that agent will mislead others. Every month, thousands of home-sellers lose thousands of dollars due to the incompetence or the dishonesty of real estate agents. You can help to stop it *if you complain*. But if you do nothing, then the agent who cheated or misled you will be free to cheat others. (Perhaps the reason you were cheated was because other home-sellers who had been cheated before you, did nothing.)

Many problems in the real estate industry are caused because agents have too much influence. The agents protect each other at the expense of consumers.

The advice in this book will protect you and your family from the stress of making the common real estate mistakes. It will save you thousands of dollars when you sell your home.

You can now return to Chapter 1 and begin to interview agents with the full confidence that you now have the knowledge to find the best agent to sell your home.

TEN VITAL POINTS FOR SELLING YOUR HOME

and avoiding all the costly mistakes made by most home-sellers.

1. Invest in a valuation and seek independent legal advice.

2. Choosing an agent is your most important decision.

3. The agent must be a skilled negotiator. Do not hire an agent you do not like.

4. Choosing the method of sale is your second most important decision.

5. The best method of sale is the 'Smart-Sale' method. Give your home to the best agent by 'Private Treaty' under an exclusive agreement with a written guarantee of 'no charges until sold'.

6. Make sure your home presents well. A warm feeling wins the hearts of buyers.

7. Start with a high asking price. Never start low.

8. Reduce the asking price until you receive the highest selling price.

9. Do not demand useless or ineffective activity, such as advertising to 'non-buyers' or open inspections.

10. Only sell when you can afford to do so.

PART THREE
Winning
in
Real Estate

Chapter Twelve

ETHICS IN REAL ESTATE

Salus populi suprema est lex.

"The people's good is the highest law."

Agent Benefit Systems V's Client Benefit Systems

◆

When You Are a Seller and a Buyer

◆

Inside Real Estate (briefly)

◆

How Everyone Can Win in Real Estate

In 1943, a 69 year old writer, Somerset Maugham, published an essay on Virtue.[1] He said most people accept the importance of the virtues of integrity and self-sacrifice, but this is not enough to weigh against the powerful motives of self-interest.

Maugham said that people can only do what is right when the correct virtues have become habits. And these habits must be so strong that acting upon them becomes instinctive.

In real estate, the opposite has occurred. Thousands of agents, focussed on self-interest, have developed systems and habits which are so bad they can't help hurting sellers and buyers. They do the wrong thing instinctively.

Self-interest is not good business, because what is wrong for clients will ultimately be wrong for agents. The focus on self causes the destruction of self.

The real estate industry, despite its image, is battling. Each year hundreds of agents go broke and thousands of salespeople quit. In one state, recruits are informed at their entrance course that ninety percent of them will not last more than one year in real estate.[2]

There are two ways to measure success in business - client satisfaction and profit. On both of these measures, the real estate industry fails.

Agent Benefit Systems V's Client Benefit Systems

The two systems in real estate are agent benefit systems and client benefit systems. Ninety percent of real estate systems are agent benefit systems. And that's why ninety percent of agents have low profits and why ninety percent of consumers do not trust agents. Their self-interest hurts their clients and it hurts them.

> "...any system that is not good for everyone always fails."

If anyone criticises the agent benefit systems or suggests that client benefits should be increased, many agents respond with abuse. *"You are destroying the industry!"*

But any system that is not good for everyone always fails. And real estate is failing. It is failing its clients and it is failing its agents. For agents to make more profits they must do more for their clients. They have no choice other than to destroy their old systems which focus on themselves and create new systems which focus on clients.

Once the clients are happy, the profits will follow.

Whether you are selling or buying a home, always look for agents who use client benefit systems. They are easy to recognise. They care about you first.

It shows in everything they do.

When You Are a Seller And a Buyer

Most buyers one day become sellers. And most sellers buy again. This is why it is important to have systems where everyone wins - sellers and buyers. It is not much good winning as a buyer and then losing as a seller. The best situation is to win in all situations.

Winning in real estate does not mean someone has to lose. It means doing the best for yourself without hurting anyone else. As Wesley Harris, the former Salvation Army Commissioner said: *"The most profitable deal is one in which no-one loses."*

> "Winning in real estate does not mean someone has to lose."

The best agents do not have any losers - either sellers or buyers. The best agents get the best prices for the sellers and the best homes for the buyers.

Do You Sell First or Buy First?

If you want to sell your home and buy another, which comes first - selling or buying? There seem to be dangers whatever you choose.

The advice you receive from agents is often the advice which is best for the agent. The agents will tell you to sell first if they are going to be the selling agent or, if you are thinking of buying from them, you may be told to buy first. If you sell first, you have nowhere to live. If you buy first, you may not be able to sell - unless you sell fast and cheap.

So, what do you do - sell first or buy first?

The answer is neither: **Do not sell first and... Do not buy first.**

Instead, do them *both at the same time*.

It's the safest way. Plus, it gives you complete control with low pressure.

Here's how you sell and buy at the same time:

First, you place your home for sale (NOT FOR AUCTION - it is almost impossible to sell and buy at the same time with auction). It is easier for agents when sellers are forced to sell. But you are not going to be forced to do anything; you are going to do it your way. And you are going to win - without having anyone else lose.

Confidence

Here is a point which should give you great confidence - **placing your home for sale does not mean selling your home.** If you put your home for sale, you can - at any time before you sign a contract with a buyer - change your mind. You are entitled to do this because, as the owner, you can sell under *your conditions*. Your condition is that you will not sell before you find another home to buy.

Your goal is to sign the contract to sell your home at the same time as you sign the contract to buy another home. This is a common method and if your agent can't help you, your lawyer will.

Once your home is for sale, your agent will tell buyers that it is a condition of sale that you must find another home. Agents may claim that this will deter buyers, but this is not true. It is a strategy often used by the best agents to protect home-sellers.

Before you find a buyer for your home, you may be tempted to go and look at other homes. If so, that's fine, provided that you remember this point - **inspecting homes for sale does not mean buying a home.** If you see a home you really like, then make it a condition of your purchase that you will not buy until you have sold.

If you are genuine in your intentions - the best agents will understand this and they will look after you. They will agree that the best thing for you is to get the highest price possible for your home *at the same time as you buy the home which best suits you.*

They will explain your condition of sale to buyers and they will explain your condition of purchase to sellers. Do not worry. This will work as long as you are not tempted.

The Golden Rule is: **Do not sign anything without speaking with your lawyer** - or an independent and trusted adviser - first.

One final point: Be reasonable, especially when it comes to price. Some people make the mistake of holding out for too high a price on the home they are selling and they lose the home they want to buy. Always measure both prices together - the home you sell and the home you buy.

A Summary of Selling and Buying Together

The solution to selling and buying at the same time can be summed up in four simple stages.

Stage 1. Find a Buyer.

Finding a buyer for your home does not mean selling your home. It means you have found a buyer who will accept your condition of you finding another home before you sell.

Stage 2. Find a Home.

Finding a home does not mean buying a home. It means you have found a home where the seller will accept your condition of selling your home before you buy.

Stage 3. Match Finances.

Once you have found a buyer for your home and you have found a home to buy, you have to make sure there is enough money from your sale to cover your purchase.

Stage 4. Sell old home. Buy new home.

This is the final stage of selling and buying at the same time. It is the perfect solution with no risk and low stress. If the finances match, you sign a contract to sell at the same time as you sign a contract to buy.

Make sure, of course, that the conditions of both contracts are the same, especially the 'time conditions'. You don't want to spend two weeks in a motel. A good real estate lawyer will help you.

Selling and buying, at the same time, can be simple, safe and pleasant.

Inside Real Estate (briefly)

Repeating the Errors

> "If honest people do not have happy clients, their conscience troubles them."

Most agents copy each other. If one agent offers a discount, another one will offer a bigger discount. If one agent places big advertisements in a newspaper, another one will place bigger advertisements. If one does auctions, another agent will do auctions.

At the end of each month, they look at the hours they have worked and the profit they have made and they see the same result - high numbers of hours and low profits.

Their solution is to repeat - even increase - the same errors in the hope that one day everything will work out. But it doesn't. Low profits and low client satisfaction are the two results the real estate industry does not talk about publicly. Privately, it is their greatest concern.

Incompetence or Dishonesty

There is a difference between being dishonest and being incompetent. Many honest people do incompetent things. And nowhere is this more evident than in real estate.

But when good people continue to use bad systems and get bad results, the competency of those people must be questioned. It is said that one of the signs of insanity is a person who repeats the same actions and expects different results.

Agents have different views on their problems. Some cling to old systems for no other reason than "this is the way everyone does it." Others are fed up with low profits, high hours and low client satisfaction. They are eager to change.

But there is something else which is far more important than profits. It's the *feeling* about what is done. If honest people do not have happy clients, their conscience troubles them.

One long-established agent brought his son into the business. Years later, they had a heated conversation about the ethics of auctions. The agent said, *"Our auctions sell and our clients are happy. I've been doing auctions for 20 years."*

> "...it is hard for anyone to argue the merits of a dishonest system without looking foolish."

The son replied, *"Yes Dad, but in the years I have been with you, how many homes have we sold for less than we could have sold them for?"* The answer was "Many of them."

This agent now focuses totally on client benefits. And his business is thriving. After forty years of trading, his agency is setting records in sales volume, profits and best of all, client satisfaction.

Honest people are capable of being highly competent provided they focus on what is best for their clients. They also need a quality which Churchill described as the most important of all - courage. It takes great courage to admit that you are wrong and that maybe your systems are based on self-interest.

Dishonest agents use 'legal' as their standard. It is legal to receive kickbacks so they do it. It is legal to have 'dummy bidders' so they do it. But, as most real estate systems show, legal does not always mean honest.

In his book, *Character is Destiny - The Value of Personal Ethics in Everyday Life*, Professor Russell Gough, says:

"Being ethical is never just a matter of being a good rule-follower. It's exceedingly more than that. Rules and laws by their very nature usually prescribe, at best, only minimum standards of ethical behaviour."

Professor Gough recommends we tell ourselves,

"While I must have the character to play by the rules, I must also have the character to do the right thing when the rules don't help. If I want to have the character to strive for ethical excellence, then I must have the character to draw the line when there is no line drawn."

Real estate systems which focus on agent-benefits might be legal but they certainly don't sit on the right side of the ethical line for consumers. And it is hard for anyone to argue the merits of a dishonest system without looking foolish.

Ego and Advertising

The late Hal Geneen, of ITT Sheraton, said that the greatest danger in business was ego.[3]

Ego does huge damage to the real estate industry. Unable to pay for the massive costs of self-promotion, agents have transferred these costs to consumers so that tens of millions of dollars pour into the major newspapers. But the number of sales have not increased; only the number of advertisements have increased.

In addition to kickbacks, some newspapers offer 'sweet-heart' deals to agents such as free personal advertising, corporate boxes and champagne at sporting events, or sponsorship of seminars and advertising awards.

With the newspapers making more money from real estate sales than real estate agents, there is little chance of them exposing this consumer wastage.

The real estate industry is addicted to ego advertising with many agents putting more focus on looking good than on doing good. They feed their egos with the money of home-sellers who can't afford these huge costs.

But the newspapers are the big winners - their revenues have soared thanks to the incompetence and ego of thousands of real estate agents. And all at the expense of home-sellers.

Staff Recruitment and Treatment

A common method of rewarding sales staff is by 'commission only'. By not offering salaries, real estate agents believe that salespeople do not cost anything. If they make a sale, they get paid and the office gets paid. If they don't make a sale, they get nothing. They starve.

This method of recruiting and rewarding does untold damage to the real estate industry.

Jeanne and Herbert Greenberg are the authors of *Creating Sales Team Excellence*, a book which examines why salespeople succeed or fail. They say, *"'No-cost' salespeople are actually costing a great deal. The lack of salary creates one of the greatest dis-services to the industry, because it makes the hiring decision so easy. The real estate industry, more than many others, needs careful selection of salespeople if the profession is to reach the level of respect its importance deserves."*

> "...many agents do not consider salespeople important enough to warrant a fair salary."

Selling a family home *is* an important job. Yet many agents do not consider salespeople important enough to warrant a fair salary.

Imagine saying to a person with a family, *"Come and work in our real estate office. If you don't sell anything you won't be paid."* Many people, who could be a great asset to the real estate industry, are not interested in such conditions.

221

If employees are treated badly, they will treat clients and colleagues badly, or they will leave.

Many agents lose their most ethical and promising people because of the culture within their offices. These people either leave real estate - and spread the word about the bad ethics of agents - or they search for an office with a good culture and high ethical standards. And this is no easy task because many of the best real estate offices have strict recruitment standards. They will not hire salespeople with real estate 'experience' because of the bad habits they have acquired.

> "If a salesperson is being paid 'commission only', the interest of the sellers often comes second to the interests of the salesperson."

An example of the behaviour many new salespeople witness is the way buyers' offers are given to sellers. Sometimes there will be two buyers interested in a home. One buyer will offer more than the other. However, the highest offer is not necessarily given to the seller. The offer given to the seller is the one which was obtained first. The amount of the offer comes second to the *time* of the offer. This is done to protect the salespeople. It's called "first one in gets the sale."

If a salesperson is being paid 'commission only', the interest of the sellers often comes second to the interests of the salesperson. There is a saying, "*Necessity can make the most honest person a knave.*"

Shocked salespeople who say, "*But what about the seller*", are often told to be quiet and stop being silly because this is "business."

It may be business but it is another example of dishonest business being created from systems based entirely on self-interest.

As one agent, who pays salaries and bonuses, said, "*If you treat people like beasts, they act like beasts. But if you offer a high salary, good conditions and quality training, you will attract and keep the finest people.*"

Education and Training

It is an old real estate joke: New salespeople get three things - a phone, a desk and a month. They learn by watching the 'old dogs' in the office.

In South Australia, new salespeople must have a nominated 'trainer' at the office. The only qualifications the trainer needs is more than two years real estate sales experience, thus guaranteeing the spread of bad habits.

Instead of focusing on what home-sellers want, typical real estate training focuses on how agents can talk people into things they neither want nor need. As one agent explained, "*I wasted four years of my life talking home-sellers into something they didn't want (auctions).*"

The examination questions in sales courses include: '*Explain why auctions are the best way to sell real estate.*'

If the correct answer, *Auctions are not the best way to sell real estate*, is given, the answer is marked as wrong. The student fails. You only have to look at the 'end product' to see the quality of training given to typical agents.

> "The most basic study of ethics and client care is lacking from the common real estate courses."

Consumer complaints are so high that some training courses are now teaching agents how to avoid being sued. One course, conducted by the Real Estate Institute of New South Wales is simply titled: '**AUCTIONS - AVOID BEING SUED**'.[4] The course advertises "NEW" information, such as 'The law relating to auctions'. To state that the 'law' of auctions is a new topic is a staggering admission.

No Real Estate Institute course is called '*How to sell real estate ethically and have happy clients*'.

Ethics Education

Most of the ethical problems in real estate can be linked directly to the training and education of agents and salespeople. Training programs based on self-interest systems can never lead to client satisfaction.

The most basic study of ethics and client care is lacking from the common real estate courses.

It is amazing that the real estate industry does not consider ethical conduct to be important enough to teach or that ideas from other ethical and successful industries are not studied.

In his article, *Corporate Ethics*, business writer, Manuel Velasquez says that *"ethics requires self-sacrifice"* but in the short-term, ethical behaviour may not be rewarding.[5]

And here lies the root of the problem. Real Estate Agents have short-term relationships with their clients. Typically, they see clients as 'one-hit' propositions. The need for repeat business in real estate is not the same as for a restaurant. If restaurant patrons are given food-poisoning, they do not come back. But when sellers and buyers are financially or emotionally poisoned, it is too late - the sale has been made and the agent has been paid.

The reputation of all agents suffers every time a client suffers from unethical behaviour. Unethical behaviour is unprofitable no matter what the business or how long the relationship with the client lasts.

Velasquez says that ethics is a "valuable business asset" and that companies need to be ethical in all ways - to their staff and to their clients. If not, the employees will treat the company and the clients badly, there will be a high turnover of staff and more expense to the company. This is exactly the situation in the real estate industry.

"Firms that maintain high ethical standards in their treatment of customers find that customers are willing to pay a premium to the firm

for good treatment. Such firms have been able to increase their market share while raising their prices. Thus, a commitment to ethics can pay handsomely."

The article mentions companies such as Hewlett-Packard, whose high ethical standards have been the foundation of its spectacular success. Hewlett-Packard measures its success in terms of client satisfaction before profits.

In the book, *The HP Way*, there is a story about the early days of Hewlett-Packard and how the directors of the company deliberately slowed sales in order to focus on high client satisfaction. They put ethics before profit.

Ethics is good business. And ethics begins with how people are taught to act. It begins with education and training.

Silencing its Critics

Unfortunately for consumers, the real estate industry tends to 'cover-up' rather than 'fix-up', as this next story shows.

Article 3 of the Real Estate Institute Code of Ethics states: *"A member must never publicly criticise a fellow agent."* To speak out about bad practices is to run the risk of expulsion.

This is what happened to one agent in South Australia who distributed a book on how to select a good agent. Several agents complained to the Real Estate Institute. He protested that the book was accurate and that home-sellers loved it. *"It might be true,"* came the reply, *"but you are not allowed to say it."*[6]

When he refused to withdraw the book, he was expelled for *"participating in conduct detrimental to the interest of the Institute."* He was found guilty and expelled. But it didn't stop there.

The Institute faxed a memo to all its member agents in South Australia with the heading *"Member Expelled for Breach of Ethics"*. This memo was then displayed in agents' windows and delivered anonymously to the agent's clients. Here was an agent, who, by being loyal to clients had to be disloyal to agents and who was then expelled from the Institute for "breach of (their) ethics". Such a happening can only be described as amazing.

In 1999, another Real Estate Institute contacted its public relations company with instructions to "mount an on-going campaign" against the author of this book. When asked why, the reply given was *"He is too honest in exposing the bad systems and is upsetting our members."*[7]

This is the real estate industry in Australia today. This cult of 'internal protection' causes many honest agents to either get out of real estate or remain quiet - at least publicly - for fear of retribution.

How Everyone Can Win in Real Estate

We can all win in real estate when we use the **golden rule of life** - do to others what you want others to do to you. Sellers can achieve the right price, buyers can find the right home and agents can be paid for being the person whose high standards helped make winning possible.

> "People who are ethical in their dealings with others are the true winners in life."

People who are ethical in their dealings with others are the true winners in life. And most people truly want to be ethical - they want to do the right thing by others.

Sellers and buyers don't want to cheat each other, nor do they want to be cheated. If someone has to lose for you to win, then, one day, you will have to lose so that someone else can win. Life is like that. Dishonesty does not lead to winning.

In real estate, too many people are losing. It is rare that sellers, buyers and agents all win when a home is sold.

Ethics

Ethics in real estate must begin from within the real estate industry. Agents have much work to do if they are to regain the trust of sellers and buyers.

Ethics in real estate is not easy. It requires agents to accept the irrefutable evidence that many of their systems hurt consumers. And that's what most agents won't do.

But, as the ethics professor, Russell Gough says, *"What kind of people are we if we don't have the character to own up to our own shortcomings and responsibilities?"*

The mistakes made by real estate consumers are caused by the bad systems and poor ethics typically used in the real estate industry. It is one of our greatest national scandals. And it is a hidden scandal. If the real estate industry won't accept it, there should be a major *independent* enquiry into the millions of dollars being lost by home-sellers.

But, when Governments want to know what is happening in real estate, they ask the Real Estate Institutes. This is absurd because, as has been repeatedly stated in this book, **Real Estate Institutes are Real Estate Agents.**

> "There should be a major independent enquiry into the millions of dollars being lost by home-sellers."

The Real Estate Institutes have had an entire century to bring ethics into real estate. As much as they may have tried, and as well meaning and ethical as some of their members may be, they have failed. *Ninety percent of consumers do not trust agents.*

Real Estate Institutes do not represent consumers. To have Board Members of Institutes openly boasting that kickbacks from newspapers pay for their personal expenses such as lease payments on expensive cars, as the people who advise Government on real estate issues, is a scandalous conflict of interest.

Sellers and buyers are sick of placing their trust in agents and being ripped off or having their hearts broken.

Knowledge

If you are a home-seller, you now have the knowledge to avoid mistakes which cost you thousands of dollars. If you are a home-buyer, you have the knowledge to protect yourself and find the home you want at a price you can afford. If you are an agent, you know how to take care of consumers.

Ethics in real estate will help all Australians become winners in real estate. It will make the business of buying or selling a home the wonderful experience it is meant to be. It will help more home-owners live happily ever after.

And that is why this book was written.

Letter to Home-Seller

RE: AUCTION QUOTE

Suggested Letter to home-sellers if you feel the agent is misleading you about the likely selling price of a home offered for auction.

WARNING: If you do not receive a response to this letter, look for another home.

Dear [Insert Name of Owner]

We are interested in buying your property which is for sale by auction on [Insert Date].

The agent gave us an estimate of the likely sale price which is within the price range we can afford.

However, we are very worried.

We are not sure if the agent is <u>under</u>-estimating the price. We asked the agent to confirm the estimate in writing, but this request was refused. This makes us nervous as it might mean that the price we have been given is not correct.

If the most we can afford to pay is less than you want, there is no point in us spending money on legal fees or searches or inspections, because we will be losing several hundred dollars.

Can you help us?

All we want to know is that we have some <u>chance</u> of buying your property because we really like it.

The agent's estimated price was [state agent's verbal estimate].

We would really appreciate your comments and hope to hear from you as soon as possible.

Our contact number is [insert all numbers and details].

Thank you.

Yours sincerely

[Your Name/s]

Letter to Agent

To reduce the risk of Gazumping

Suggested Letter to agent to be used if you are interested in buying – or negotiating to buy - a home, and you are worried the agent may sell it to another buyer without informing you, thus giving you no chance to buy.

<u>ADVICE</u>: The agent should sign a copy of this letter.

Dear [Insert Name of Agent]

RE: [Address of Property]

As discussed with you, we are very interested in purchasing the above property.

We are hoping to be able to sign an unconditional contract to purchase when [Insert details – such as "negotiations are complete"; "searches and inspections have been done"; "the auction is held"; "finance is arranged" etc].

We are aware that there is no legal obligation upon us, or the owner of the property, until such time as we have both signed an unconditional contract.

However, we are concerned that the home may be sold to another buyer without us being told, which would therefore deny us any chance to buy.

The purpose of this letter is to ask that you confirm the following:

1. <u>The property will NOT be sold to another buyer without us being told</u>. We want to, at least, have the opportunity to match or <u>better</u> any other offer should any other buyer become interested.

2. We also request that you inform the owner of our interest and that we have written this letter to you.

If you agree to these two points, please indicate your agreement by signing a copy of this letter.

Thank you.

Yours sincerely

[Your Name]

Letter to Auction Agent

To cancel a sale by Auction

Dear [Insert Name of Agent]

RE: [Address of Property]

This letter is to confirm that we do NOT want to sell our home by auction.

Since signing the auction authority we have become aware of a number of points which you did not tell us about. We now believe an auction is not the best way for us to achieve the highest price.

Also, we will not be allowing any more public open inspections of our home.

Please remove your auction sign as soon as possible and cancel all auction advertising immediately. With regard to the money we paid you for advertising, please arrange a refund of the unused portion of this money. No more of our money is to be spent on the auction campaign.

We are prepared to meet with you, in person, to discuss a better method of sale.

We trust that you will respect our decision, which is irrevocable.

Thank you.

Yours sincerely

[Your Name]

Letter to Auction Agent

To cancel the Auction and dismiss the agent

ADVICE: Add or delete any points which
may or may not apply in your case.

Dear [Insert Name of Agent]

RE: [Address of Property]

This letter is to confirm that we no longer wish to sell our home
by auction and we no longer want your agency to handle the sale
of our home.

Since our first meeting with you, a number of things have disturbed us:

1. The price quoted to us at the time we signed the auction
   agreement was, in our opinion, a ploy to persuade us to
   choose auction.

2. We believe we are the victims of a process known as
   'conditioning' because you are constantly referring to prices
   which are much lower than you told us before we
   signed up for auction.

3. Your agency is receiving a kickback on our advertising
   money.

4. Our advertising money is being used to promote your agency.

5. The price being quoted to prospective buyers is well below
   our minimum price and this is attracting buyers who cannot
   afford to buy our home. It is also misleading the buyers.

6. If our home fails to sell at auction we will lose all the money
   we have paid for advertising, but your agency will have
   benefited by increased profile and the kickback from the
   advertising which you were not intending to pass on to us.

7. If our home fails to sell at auction, it will almost certainly
   damage our chance of a good price.

We believe that the conduct of your agency has been highly deceptive and greatly misleading. We therefore wish to terminate your authority to act as our agent.

We request that you do the following:

1. Remove your auction sign.

2. Return all keys and all documentation relating to our home.

3. Cancel all auction advertising and refund our money including the amount of any kickback you are to receive from the newspapers.

We trust that you will not make this matter any more unpleasant and that you will attend to these requests immediately and confirm in writing that you no longer have our authority to be our agent.

Our decision is final and irrevocable.

Yours sincerely

[Your Name]

AUTHOR'S COMMENT

If you have never sold by auction, you may find it hard to accept that a letter such as this would ever need to be written. But thousands of home-sellers have experienced every one of these points. This is the letter which would have saved them from losing thousands of dollars. Hopefully, you will never need to use it.

Australian Property Institute

API NATIONAL SECRETARIAT 6 Campion Street **DEAKIN, ACT.** 2600. Tel: (02) 6282 2411 Fax: (02) 6285 2194 Email: national@propertyinstitute.com.au	**API - ACT Division** 6 Campion Street, **DEAKIN, ACT.** 2600. Tel: (02) 6282 5541 Fax: (02) 6282 5536 Email: act.div@propertyinstitute.com.au
API - WA Division (27 Charles Street, **SOUTH PERTH, WA.** 6151) Tel: (08) 9474 2784 Fax: (08) 9474 1157 Email: apiwa@propertyinstitute.com.au	**API - SA Division** (1st Floor, 187 Fullarton Road, **DULWICH, SA.** 5065.) Tel: (08) 8431 9411 Fax: (08) 8431 9422 Email: API@maccoul.com.au
API - TAS Division (Floor 1, 25 Davey Street, **HOBART, TAS.** 7000. Tel: (03) 6224 1324 Fax: (03) 6224 3441 Email: sandra@eisa.net.au	**API - VIC Division** 10 Beach Street, **PORT MELBOURNE, VIC.** 3207. Ph: (03) 9646 1977 Fax: (03) 9646 4635 Email: secretariat@vic.propertyinstitute.com.au
API - QLD Division 2nd Floor, Suite 202, 131 Leichhardt Street, **SPRING HILL, QLD.** 4000 Tel: (07) 3832 3139 Fax: (07) 3839 0438 Email: qld@propertyinstitute.com.au	**API - NSW Division** Level 3, 60 York Street, **SYDNEY, NSW.** 2000 Tel: (02) 9299 1811 Fax: (02) 9299 1490 Email: nsw@propertyinstitute.com.au

Further Reading

In the world of business, you can tell the readers from the non-readers. You can see it in the way they treat their clients and their staff.

Good books enrich your life – both personally and professionally. They contain so many ideas and so many solutions that it is a wonder any person can manage life without them.

The following books can help all business people improve their lives and the lives of everyone with whom they do business. I recommend them all.

Lenz, Vicki	**The Saturn Difference** **- Creating Customer Loyalty in your Company**
Gough, Russell W.	**Character is Destiny.** **The Value of Personal Ethics in Everyday Life**
Cairnes, Margot	**Approaching the Corporate Heart**
Roddick, Anita	**Body and Soul**
Brinker, Norman	**On the Brink** **- The Life and Leadership of Norman Brinker**
Maihafer, Harry, Col J.	**Brave Decisions – Moral Courage**
Wilson, Robert A. (Ed)	**Character Above All**
Geneen, Harold S.	**Managing**
Madsen, Peter. Shafritz, Jay	**Essentials of Business Ethics**
De Becker, Gavin	**The Gift of Fear**
Collins, James C. & Porras, Jerry I.	**Built To Last**
Packard, David	**The HP Way** **- How Bill Hewlett and I Built Our Company**
Hartley, Anne	**Debt Free – How to Get Out of Debt, Stay Out of Debt and Still Live the Life You Want**
Preston, Noel	**Understanding Ethics**
Greenberg, Jeanne and Herbert	**Creating Sales Team Excellence**
McCullough, David	**Truman**
Tracy, Brian	**Maximum Achievement**
Bell, Anita	**Your Mortgage and How To Pay it Off in Five Years by Someone who did it in Three**
Mackay, Harvey	**Swim With The Sharks** **Without Being Eaten Alive**
Whittaker, Noel	**Golden Rules of Wealth**

Notes and Reference Sources

Introduction

1.
Property: 10 Tuckwell Road, Castle Hill
Seller: Walter Clift
Buyer: Peter and Beverley McLaughlin
Price: $285,000
Date of settlement: February 28, 1994
Seller: Peter and Beverley McLaughlin
Buyer: DGC Investments Pty Ltd
Price: $420,000
Date of settlement: February 28, 1994
As reported to author by District Zone Chairman of the Real Estate Institute of NSW.

In addition to the commission charged to Clift, the agent received a commission of $9,500 from McLaughlin. In 1996, the agent commenced defamation proceedings against the author of this book following comments at a real estate seminar. To date (December 1999), nothing further has eventuated.

2.
Property: 12 Mi Mi Road, Algate, SA.
Scheduled for auction September 25, 1999.
Agent's quoted selling price was $240,000 to $250,000. Buyers, Paul and Lyn Busuttil prepared to pay at least $600,000. Property sold prior to auction to another buyer for $520,000 without Paul and Lyn being notified. On Wednesday October 6, the agent published an advertisement with the heading, 'SOLD WELL ABOVE MARKET PRICE – AUCTIONS WORK!'. Below the heading was a list of 15 properties, the first of which was Mi Mi Road.
Footnote: In November 1999, the buyer who paid $520,000, was "considering" re-selling the home to Paul and Lyn for $600,000.

3.
For several years, the author has asked home-owners two questions: 1) How much did you pay for your home? And, 2) How much would you have paid? The difference has averaged $10,000.

4.
In July 1999, the Cumberland Newspaper Group banned advertisements for the booklet '18 Costly Mistakes made by Home-Sellers'. The reason given was that this booklet was "unsuitable for publication". In August 1999, The Homes Pictorial banned the same booklet. The reason given was "the aggressive response" from other agents.

Chapter One

1.
Job Loss, It's a family affair. Alix Bradfield, Jill Jukes and Ruthan Rosenberg.
ISBN 0-85091-553-8

Chapter Three

1.
Your Mortgage Magazine, Spring 1999 issue, researched the difference between quoted prices and selling prices. The article *'What they say and what you pay.'* revealed that the average difference in Sydney was 15.26 percent. In Melbourne, the difference was 20.73 percent.

2.

Money, Channel 9, Wednesday August 6, 1997.

3.

The Age, Melbourne. Saturday September 18, 1999. 'Buyers' Advocates Criticised'.

4.

From: Noel Whittaker To: Readers of Noel Whittaker's Books. Saturday September 25 1999 1:05 am Subject: This week's newsletter. Capital growth is never guaranteed – remember the adage wherever there is a chance of capital gain there is a chance of capital loss!!

5.

An article in *The Sun-Herald*, Sunday October 3, 1999, headed 'Nightmare Property Deal' is typical of scores of articles written about 'marketers' cheating consumers. This article told of Alan and Jan Bailey who were contacted in 1995 by a tele-marketer and invited to an investment seminar. They were given a free flight to the Gold Coast and a night at a five star hotel. They purchased a townhouse for $179,000 which they were told would be "projected to increase to $263,000 within five years." However, in 1999, Alan and Jan were unable to sell the townhouse even for $130,000 through a local agent.

The Queensland Office of Fair Trading commented, "The effect of the purchase of over-priced assets is that many people relatively close to the end of their working lives are incurring large capital losses and putting their current and future financial security at risk."

The marketing company in this case was the Epic Group (formerly the Coral Reef Group). This company reputedly sold more than 2,000 properties under similar investment deals in 1998.

6.

Open letter sent from Melbourne franchise network urging agents to "Act now or be silenced".

In *The Australian Financial Review*, Friday October 8, 1999, an article headed 'Battle for lucrative real estate dollars' said that agents face losing at least $10 billion turnover to financial planners. While this figure – which refers to the selling price turnover not the commission turnover – seems exaggerated, it nevertheless shows the concern within the real estate industry.

Chapter Five

1.

Real Estate Institute of Victoria, Auction Interest Group Seminar. Topic: "What Do You Say to the Vendor when the Purchaser is About to Sign the Contract and Has a Bank Cheque For More Than the 10%? (meaning he/she would have paid more)".

Chapter Six

1.

In areas where prices are low – notably, the country – a fee of eight or ten percent on the first few thousand dollars of the selling price is common and accepted.

2.

Australian Bureau of Statistics. 1996.

3.

A Real Estate Institute represents its members who are all real estate agents. The common perception that Institutes represent real estate consumers is wrong. While many agents *are* interested in protecting consumers, it can be very frustrating for these agents to witness the attitudes of many Institute directors.

Kids Alive
Do the Five

1. Fence the pool

2. Shut the gate

3. Teach your kids to swim, it's great

4. Supervise, watch your mate

5. And learn how to resuscitate

Laurie Lawrence

Each year in Australia many children drown in backyard swimming pools. Please 'Do The Five' and keep our kids alive. Thank you.